THE
# KNOWLEDGE
# ACTIVISTS
HANDBOOK

# VICTOR **NEWMAN**

THE
# KNOWLEDGE
# ACTIVISTS
HANDBOOK

ADVENTURES FROM THE **KNOWLEDGE TRENCHES**

JET LIBRARY

CAPSTONE

Copyright © Victor Newman, 2002

The right of Victor Newman to be identified as the author of this book has been asserted in accordance with the Copyright, Designs and Patents Act 1988

First Published 2002 by

Capstone Publishing Limited (A Wiley Company)
8 Newtec Place
Magdalen Road
Oxford
OX4 1RE
United Kingdom
http://www.capstoneideas.com

CIP catalogue records for this book are available from the British Library and the US Library of Congress

ISBN 1-84112-320-X

Typeset in 10/13 pt Minion
by Sparks Computer Solutions Ltd
http://www.sparks.co.uk
Printed and bound by
TJ International Ltd, Padstow, Cornwall

Substantial discounts on bulk quantities of Capstone Books are available to corporations, professional associations and other organizations. For details telephone Capstone Publishing on (+44-1865-798623), fax (+44-1865-240941) or email (info@wiley-capstone.co.uk).

This book is dedicated to my family: my wife, Diana, and our children, Philippa and Thomas. Thank you for teaching me so much.

*Victor Newman*

# Contents

# Introduction to

# *The Knowledge Activist's*

# *Handbook*

The role of the knowledge activist is to be unreasonable, to identify and combine those small grains of truth with the potential to create a pearl. This book demonstrates through the medium of storytelling how individuals can combine emotion and reflection to create their own knowledge. This is not intended to be an academic book. The idea is to attack the conspiracy of tedium around KM literature, to be provocative, counter-cultural, to turn ideas on their heads and to entertain whilst telling stories that offer insights and concrete strategies.

This is a book for busy people who want to cut to the chase and have some fun at the same time. Being a knowledge activist means deciding to make thinking about knowledge a personal activity. I wrote to encourage individuals to consider thinking their own thoughts about knowledge, through reflecting on their own experience and mining its potential nuggets.

Over the last three years I have been writing the kind of KM literature that I and my business colleagues would like to have read ourselves. The style is critical and yet pragmatic and to the point. The book is a collection of pieces varying between 700–1500 words a chapter. Some are thematically connected and bundled into the five sections. Each piece includes stories of personal consulting experiences and ends with at least 3–5 punchlines or 'implications' for the reader in terms of what they need to remember or do, for themselves.

Whilst the book is organized to be read from front to back, I would encourage a loose pick and mix approach. The provocative nature of the chapter titles encourages the reader to dive first into those chapters whose titles strike their fancy – and then to gradually colonize the text, using the margins to make their own annotations and perhaps document their own conclusions that are bound to differ from mine.

Being a knowledge activist means choosing to think about knowledge, how we use it and how it works, with a definite attitude. And doing something about it.

*Victor Newman*

# 1
# Developing Personal Knowledge

# 1.1

# Strong Concept

*The most distinctive quality of a strong concept is that it does not seem familiar.*[1]

My career as a 'knowledge activist' began at the end of 1997 when I realized that knowledge management had the potential for ending the management tendency to worship and purchase contextual problem-solving techniques that tended to obsolesce in the same, predictable way. This Coyote-like acquisition of new, more complex technologies to pursue the same old Roadrunner meant that consultants were sharpening their old knives even as knowledge management began to ramp up that first Fad-Model Slope whilst the parasitic lost tribes of knowledge management formed and began talking at conferences and publishing their empty books. And how they talked and published. They talked until I found that my suggestion of providing a translator as well as a signing correspondent for the deaf began to be taken seriously by conference organizers as well as audiences. And the conference folders got fatter, and the 2 × 2 matrices became even more involved.

The key to the problem was that all three lost tribes of knowledge management were convinced that they had already been doing knowledge all along and could go on with repackaging their old products without having to develop any new thinking. The customers would never notice. The lost tribe of Information Technology gave us systems that ordered structured data but failed to deliver any information, far less knowledge. The lost tribe of organizational learning refused to learn from this phenomenon; and the final lost tribe of lean production continued to write fatter books and still missed the idea at heart of their ideology being about the timing of money and little else. They all looked toward a technical solution for the shambles of the internet, and a computer-based approach that would replace the need for creativity or to think anything new at all. It is not surprising that none of these approaches worked.

But was there any alternative? The job of the knowledge activist is always to do something countercultural and creative. This activist approach attacked the issue of knowledge management in three ways: first, to try to identify a question that could open up the issue, and second, to adopt an out-of-the-box approach by shifting my perspective of knowledge management from that of an academic or a consultant to that of a CEO. I have learnt much from coaching and mentoring CEOs, and found that the pressures on their time mean that they need to more disciplined in the way they look at things than everyone else. The adoption of a CEO perspective on knowledge management had already helped to formulate simple approaches on knowledge leadership that seemed to work. I combined the open question and the CEO perspective with the third idea: reverse visualization. Instead of asking CEOs how they 'did' knowledge management, I asked them to try to visualize the symptoms of successful knowledge management and then work backwards, summarizing these symptoms into key messages.

The results seemed a little bit odd, but ultimately very useful.

Initially, the 12 CEOs kept asking me to explain what knowledge management was, and I had to refuse to answer, pointing out that it was important for them to develop their own perspective before I explained my views. I promised to explain my views after the workshop, when we had discussed the results.

In essence, they developed five messages from the exercise of visualizing successful knowledge management for themselves.

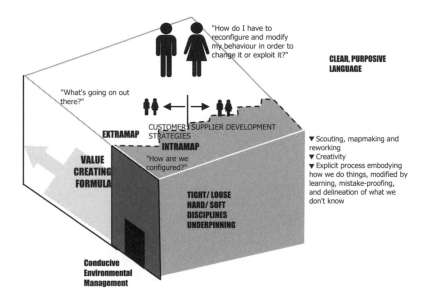

- *Language vacuum.* They didn't like the word 'knowledge' because it could mean anything to anyone and they didn't like 'Management' because it implied that whatever this 'knowledge' was, it could be managed like a passive material, stored, located physically and allocated like a physical resource. This led to thinking about a phrase like 'knowledge work' having more meaning than knowledge management.
- *Tight/Hard – Soft/Loose.* Success requires attention to everyday disciplines that focus attention and engineer mistakes out of everyday

decisions and processes. Unless there were tight/hard disciplines to manage repetitive work, not enough time could be freed up to go 'scouting': to visualize and visit alternative future scenarios to test out prevailing assumptions about the enterprise.

- *Extra/Intramaps.* A virtual technology was required to construct complementary strategy maps of the past, present and potential future. These 'extramaps' show the landscape of the global knowledge economy external to its internal knowledge economy. The 'intramap' enables the enterprise to check out its internal configuration to exploit new opportunities as well as engineer them into the environment of the extramap.

- *Visible people assets.* That individuals would understand their own responsibility for managing their personal 'brand' within the organization; in a world where there is no HR function, just individuals managing their own intellectual capital and realizing its value within the internal people market of the enterprise.

- *Applying what we know and making no repetitive mistakes.* This is the big one, to apply what we actually know! There is much that we know about where to leverage environments and mechanisms for success, and yet we ignore the cognitive equivalent of Feng-Shui unless it is sold within a brand like Neurolinguistic Programming or equivalents. Similarly, we know much about incompetence and our own potential to build our learning into everyday processes. And yet organizations end up with thousands of after-action reports and don't know how to bring them to the attention of individuals.

## Implications

1 Knowledge activism is creative and largely personal. It is the product of two complementary reinforcing processes of theft and invention, involving the generation of new models, followed by the application of these new models to old experiences, and the application of new experience to old models. All models and experiences come with a sell-by date. Having a low boredom threshold is essential.

2 Try this exercise for yourself. Pretend that you have never read this and visualize successful knowledge management for yourself, noting each symptom of success on a separate Post-it. Group these symptoms into families on a whiteboard, looking for those which are Common or Special and noticing the Missing. Fill the gaps in 'Missing', then meditate on the pattern you have created for yourself. Can you see anything new?

3 Keep applying this process until you notice something new. Then do something about it.

## Note

1 Don Simpson, quoted in Charles Fleming, *High Concept: Don Simpson and The Hollywood Culture of Excess*, Bloomsbury, 1998, p. 192.

## 1.2

# Home-grown or Tinned?

One of the interesting things about knowledge is that you often don't know what you know until someone asks you a good question.

I was approached by a group of serious-faced executives after a masterclass session and asked to give them some advice on what looked like an unique problem. They felt that they were overpaid for what they were doing and despite their excellent equity shareholdings they were considering resigning because, although their organization was a performer with admirable positioning within the Fortune 500, they felt that this success had very little to do with their individual performance. They felt that it was time to resign and go somewhere where they could make a personal impact on the success of an organization, perhaps start their own business before they got too lazy. They asked my advice. This may have been a mistake, of course, but it triggered a series of thoughts that influenced the things I found myself saying in the months that followed.

Part of my advice was that they dedicate one day a month to creating a new form of knowledge for themselves. But knowledge about what? I suggested that they start by identifying motherhood statements within their organization that they instinctively knew to be empty or meaningless, then deconstruct these using the child's repetitive 'why?' question until they got to what seemed to be the root causes and then finally go on to develop alternative, better explanations or models which could then be shared. At the very least this would create a sense of primacy, and could possibly lead to something new happening. Later on, it struck me that this is what is largely missing from knowledge literature: *how to create a new form of knowledge*. In other words, the problem of knowledge management begins with the issue of creating a new form of knowledge, and is followed with the problem of exploitation.

A common question for consulting speakers from a conference floor is the one about the extent to which 'knowledge sharing' is rewarded. The major consultancies tend to give the same message that such sharing *is* rewarded. But the issue remains: if you don't define 'knowledge' as being opportunity-based, what is being shared? How much of it is novel or just recycled? Who assigns value to it? How long will it be before desperate employees will start going to independent and bootleg knowledge suppliers on the internet for their promotional knowledge?

As Kent Greenes once said, 'make sure you have a customer for your knowledge'. Without a customer or a context for applying it, the knowledge can't be seen as valuable. The problem of context means that the time-based nature of a piece of knowledge has to be understood. As in problem-solving: you often don't know you have a problem until you see someone else's solution. So sharing knowledge isn't the problem, the real problem is expressing or creating a crisis or context for creating new forms of knowledge and supporting individuals and interest-groups in taking that knowledge to market. Knowledge sharing suggests that someone else is going to make it happen. What is usually missing in organizations is an explicit Knowledge-to-Internal-Market process (K2iM) to fast-track the application of internally-generated competitive knowledge internally, with a sister Knowledge-to-External-Market process (K2exM). With such explicit processes shared across the organization, anyone would have the potential to create a new form of knowledge and take it to market. This issue was underlined by some work I was doing on an internal creativity programme for a consultancy. I asked for case studies that demonstrated that creativity had made an impact on the bottom line. It turned out that there were few, and most had been done in spite of senior management. It seems that a better question to ask consultancies isn't how they reward knowledge sharing, but how much of their new knowledge has become an internal product that has changed the way that they work, and what examples have seen it become products sold and used by other people.

Managing knowledge is like preparing a dessert for dinner with a group of close friends. Which is likely to taste better and be the most appreciated: the dessert prepared from the fruit you grew yourself, the one with tinned fruit, or the prepared fruit dessert bought at a supermarket?

## Implications

1 Create a knowledge crisis and communicate it. Admit you don't know the answers and that the asset technology you're exploiting now won't last forever.
2 Develop and share explicit knowledge to internal and external market processes. Make these processes as basic, fundamental and available as First Aid.
3 Encourage the creation of new forms of knowledge, skunk-works knowledge prototyping and associated development of new customers.
4 Don't send your people on management development programmes, instead give them the money to invest in making their new form of knowledge work and let them keep the return. Encourage them to share the lessons of success and failure at an internal Knowledge Fair.

SECTION

1

## 1.3

# Tightrope Walking

Tightrope walkers crossing chasms between tall buildings resist the pressure from gusting winds by balancing a pole horizontally as they walk. Their balancing-pole allows them to move forward. Organizations, like tightrope walkers with their pole, must take up a position along the continuum that exists between two extremes. At one end is knowledge management, which is concerned with managing what we know about what we do. At the other end is knowledge development, which is to do with creating new forms of knowledge that introduce discontinuity and generate new market value. Knowledge management is static and tends to focus on managing knowledge around an existing process, and is invariably connected to price and risk-reduction strategies. Knowledge development is dynamic and continually redefines the knowledge worth managing and leads to the creation of new value.

**Knowledge Management**: Managing what we know about what we do (static)

**Knowledge Development**: Creating new forms of knowledge for future opportunities (dynamic, redefines useful knowledge)

SECTION

1

The price of adopting extreme positions within the continuum can be deadly. For instance, those organizations that disconnected their scenario learning activities and invested in managing knowledge around a technology and process for delivering a commodity are laying off large populations at this moment and merging operations to reduce market capacity and process costs.

Organizations that make a strategy of positioning themselves at the knowledge development extreme run the risk of having too many ideas to play with. They have succeeded in moving themselves up the global Market Capitalization Value rankings to find that investors now require last year's landmark product introduction to be succeeded by perhaps two this year, four in the following year, and have to raise the level of their game without knowing how.

Corporate management may at this point become victims of organizational groupthink. Few individuals, especially those participating in the hike in equity values, are likely to consider the possibility that this year's success was an accident. In the absence of a discrete model of the cause of the landmark product's success, they do the next best thing and begin to believe that the absence of disciplined thinking is itself a success formula that needs to be reinforced. And before you know it, you're all wearing flared trousers and sporting beards. I am always reminded of what a friend working in Apple said about the last CEO before Steve Jobs returned: 'I knew we were finished when he [the CEO] stopped wearing ties.'

Let me tell you about a recent exercise in knowledge capture. Three key individuals left a business and, prior to departure, were intensively debriefed as to what they knew. The exercise was highly therapeutic for the subjects and much useful data was recorded. It was only six months later that the debrief team realized that the slant of their questions had been misdirected. They had been asking the wrong questions. Instead of what the individuals knew, they should have asked more about their internal cause and effect models, in other words: what do you know about why we succeeded? Can you help us in modelling this process so that we can exploit it? A perennial question on the consulting skills module within the Knowledge Management and Innovation programme I used to run at Cranfield University was: 'when will I know everything?' What lies underneath this question is a natural fear of exposure on the part of the postgraduate, of appearing to be incompetent in what is seen as a harsh and unforgiving commercial environment. It is only when individuals are forced to work in alien subject areas, facilitating often introverted specialists through generic problem-solving processes, that they realize that you don't need to know everything. All you need is the ability to ask good questions, especially the repetitive, child's question: why?

I am often reminded of Groucho Marx's famous quote to the effect that he would never join any club that would accept someone like himself as a member. In the face of market success and investors' heightened expectations due to successful knowledge development and its exploitation in the form of a stable application, a similar dog-in-the-manger attitude is required to explore and understand the emergent process that delivered it, asking the simple child's question, tracking and modelling the hidden, perhaps serendipitous, process to transform it from what is not even tacit, but pre-tacit or emergent, involving many individuals, make it explicit and then manage it as a form of knowledge.

## Implications

1 Ensure that your knowledge work balances knowledge management with knowledge development.

2 The way to repeat the success that springs from the introduction of a new form of knowledge is to invest in explicitly managing the knowledge around the fractured, emergent process that got you there in the first place.

3 Continuously redefine the knowledge that is worth managing: metaphorically set fire to the business (metaphorically) and watch which bits are retrieved from the flames, and by whom.

4 Be prepared to follow Nike's strategy of deliberately choosing to slow your pace of innovation for a period in order to invest time in making explicit the fractured and emergent knowledge in your time-to-market or commercialization process.

## 1.4

# Translate, Synthesize, Connect

A consultant friend worked for an international corporation. For the first three years he worked very hard, introducing lean production techniques into the business. This meant introducing measurement systems, benchmarking methodologies and eliminating waste in many forms through involvement and empowerment. He also made recommendations that led to new information systems whose implementation he led. The arrival of the interest in the learning organization allowed him to integrate everything he had laboured over into a coherent whole. When the knowledge revolution began to grow, he was convinced that what he had been doing had been part of that revolution. But one day, after three years of hard work across the corporation's plants around the world, he was allowed a glimpse of the real business knowledge that drove the organization. And to his initial sense of disbelief, this 'real' knowledge had nothing to do with efficiency, utilization or the involvement of large numbers of people. This 'real' knowledge turned out to be about knowing when to get into a market, when to get out; how to create value in that market and manage its decline. This knowledge was shared between three key individuals and by being allowed to see it, my friend was being invited to participate in a very privileged game.

The question he kept asking himself, was: how could he have missed the real knowledge for so long? How could he have confused what turned out to be minor tactics with a strategy?

This issue of perception is exemplified when reading Sun Tzu's *Art of War*. For many readers, it is a confusing text from 512 BC written in the period known as the 'Warring States'. Modern readers of Sun Tzu's *Art of War*[1] share the same alienation effect experienced by readers of parallel texts like Machiavelli's *The Prince*, Clausewitz's *On War*, or Musashi's *A Book of Five Rings*. This disturbing alienation is an essential and deliberate part of designing knowledge to be communicated across centuries and cultures for action. This explains why such texts are not usually studied. Sun Tzu is ultimately accessible because we all imagine that we understand war, and its apparently shared context provides a basis from which to approach the text and its meaning.

A challenge I sometimes posed for MBA students was to select three Sun Tzu quotes from a collection of my favourite ten, and ask them to explain their meaning. This usually leads to stunned silence. I would then go through the ten and explain what I believe they mean. After two or three, they begin to catch on. The disappearance of an education founded on analysing texts and summarizing findings means they need some help to get going, but they get there. The next step is to invite them to shift these quotes out of their original historical context into the current business reality to create advantage or new value. Again, this is initially very confusing because no one has ever asked them to do this. They are MBA students in the MBA factory: they are here to consume what they think is knowledge, not to think for themselves or to create their own knowledge. But after a few examples they catch on, and are generally astonished at how what appeared to be a closed text, from an exotic and remote past, can have real meaning and application in today's business reality.

Later, when we examine how the Sun Tzu text actually made them *feel* when they were working on the quotes, the answer is interesting: Sun Tzu's text makes them feel scared and cold because he is telling them something from his own world; there are only two types of people in Sun Tzu, the predator and the victim. This antithesis is a common theme on high-flier management development and serious MBA programmes.

The full text of Sun Tzu has probably only four great themes worked out within the 13 chapters.

1   *Deception and disguise.* Hide your real strategy; your real strengths and weaknesses.
2   *Timing.* Always be in control of timing. International terrorists are always the first to start and to break truces. Introduce the market leader, and always kill it yourself with your own replacement.
3   *The killing ground.* Always get to the battlefield or market first to choose the best positions, channel your competition into the worst ground or least profitable markets.
4   *Movement.* When you implement your strategy, visualize it like a torrent that sweeps away boulders, don't hit just one isolated objective but a complete, winning sequence. Make it fast and last longer than they expect.

So what can we learn from books like these? First, that if they don't alienate us, make us feel uncomfortable, then they are unlikely to contain any elements of 'real' knowledge. Although few reading Sun Tzu's text have experienced war beyond films and TV reportage, there is a common shared context that enables us to imagine we understand. However, the experience is far richer for anyone who has studied military history, served as a volunteer in the military reserves, run their own business and perhaps tried to lead people to do something different. Translating Sun Tzu must be a personal process: don't buy translations, do it for yourself. When you have annotated your text, synthesize it into your own language, then try to connect your synthesis by jumping your translation into the business context. Then apply it.

By understanding how these books work, and the way they use creativity in deliberately forcing us to take something from a strange context and apply it within a familiar context, and vice versa, we can understand how real knowledge is created and how it actually works and avoid consuming commodity information. Tim Jackson's *Inside Intel*[2] and Goldratt's *The Goal*[3] are classic examples of Sun Tzu's knowledge and technique applied.

## Implications

1 Look for the 'real' knowledge, the knowledge that underpins the perpetually recycled packaging hype.
2 Don't read modern books about strategy unless they alienate you or make you feel uncomfortable.
3 Practice translating the text for its emergent message and then try shifting it to new contexts and see what happens.

## Notes

1 Samuel B. Griffith, *Sun Tzu – The Art of War*, Oxford University Press, 1971.
2 Tim Jackson, *Inside Intel*, HarperCollins, 1998.
3 Eliyahu Goldratt and Jeff Cox, *The Goal*, Gower Publishing, 1993.

1.5

# How To Go on a Dead Cat Hunt

Understanding the levels of knowledge operating within an organization is just like tracing the source of an organizational 'dead cat' (a problem that keeps re-appearing, and which no one wants to touch because it may mean confronting powerful people or values within the culture). Trying to solve this kind of problem is a useful way of defining the necessary types of knowledge that have to be successfully integrated together to manage change in an organization. Tracking down and eradicating the source of dead cat problems can take you to the heart of the organization and the knowledge that's really driving it.

When you are tracing the source of dead cat problems, it is vital to understand both the levels of knowledge and the associated language of problem solving that the organization is willing to permit.

I characterize the primary levels of knowledge encountered through hunting the source of dead cat issues as being task, followed by process, behavioural system and, finally, environmental model. Understanding the language of problem solving in an organization is key to gaining traction and building engagement at a senior level when trying to understand why things really happen, but the issue of problem-solving language has its own contradictions.

First, it is often the case that until an organization sees a solution that is being applied by a competitor, it will continue to believe that it does not have a problem to solve. So the contradiction that has to be resolved is: which comes first, the problem or the solution? Without a problem, there is no incentive to think at deeper levels of knowledge other than task. Second, the solution tends to carry with it its own jargon and problem definition that are themselves the by-product of applying a new and successful technology. Once a company recognizes a solution to a problem that it didn't even know existed, it then has to deal with attempting to understand a language that is solution- and not problem-centred. This probably explains the need to implement major changes in organizations up to three times before they actually take. The real difficulty of implementing significant change is one of linguistic translation and acquisition. If you don't have the language, you literally can't describe the problem, much less solve it. It's not surprising that organizations sometimes choose to redefine the problem as one they are already equipped to solve, and to ignore the real problem and the real knowledge gap that it faces.

Going back to the organizational problem-solving levels of task, process, behavioural system and environmental model, consultants tend to get called into organizations to solve problems that no one wants to touch. Understanding these problems involves interviewing lots of people and sometimes discovering that this problem has an archaeology all of its own. Some interviewees will smile patronizingly at the eager consultant as if to say, 'Here comes another one.' With a bit of luck, a kind interviewee will delve deep into a dusty recess and bring out a small collection of previous attempts to work on the problem. At this point, the consultant will do one of two things: become deeply depressed because they sense that they, too, are likely to meet the same fate; or decide to save a lot of time and pirate the content of their predecessors' reports for themselves.

But what has been going on? Let me explain. Essentially, what is seen by day-to-day management as a task, is actually the by-product of a process that is itself kept from working properly by someone who is being consistently rewarded for doing something stupid by someone who no longer understands how the business really works. Someone somewhere is being paid very well for making your life a mess. And they don't know it.

But problems start out as tasks; and individuals get told to just go and sort it out. Curiosity and a bit of consultant archaeology may identify the source of the repetitious problem as being a process that doesn't work as it should. At this point the process becomes the centre of attention and more fun and games begin as a problem-solving team begins to map the process, walking through political mine- and mind-fields of internal organizations based on functional knowledge, and occasionally preaching the unthinkable idea that the organization based on functional knowledge, in blindly replicating the traditional academic model, is failing the organization. After much trauma, a new process model is defined, but unless the old functional knowledge structure is wiped out and replaced by a process knowledge structure, and a new behaviour system that rewards behaviours that help the process to work properly, this new process model that was designed to destroy the repetitive task or organizational dead cat, will become a fiction and the problem will re-emerge.

My personal research and experience in Business Process Re-engineering taught me that failure was not due to the redesign of the business process but due to the failure to go to the next level and redesign the behavioural system that drives behaviours. Once the behavioural system is itself mapped and understood, its parent needs to be confronted, and this is usually a core group of very senior managers, often role models who need to be handled very carefully in order to encourage them to articulate their own personal cause and effect models of how things actually (in their own minds) work in the business. Care has to be taken at this point, because it is likely that their core, shared environmental model of cause and effect is obsolete or based on an organization or world that no longer exists. In effect their core, personal knowledge, the knowledge that has got them where they are today, may be deeply flawed. This kind of epiphany can be earth-shattering, so take care.

## Implications

1 Without shared problem-solving language and models, it is very difficult to explain new problems and specify new knowledge gaps.

2 Unless serious effort is made to identify the source of organizational dead cats, life will tend to resemble the plot of *Groundhog Day*, where every day is identical even though the protagonists are convinced it's unique.

3 Without language and commitment to building the necessary knowledge levels that prevent the manufacture of dead-cat tasks, there will never be enough time to change anything worthwhile.

4 If you really want to change an organization, work backwards through the knowledge levels, beginning at understanding the prevailing environmental model of cause and effect.

# 2
# Developing Knowledge Leadership

## 2.1

# Smell Coffee, Taste Coffee

One of my sadder consultancy assignments was to review an engineering organization's strategy and outline the way forward. The Managing Director was not sanguine about this assignment and I could tell that the board had imposed me on him very much against his wishes. Nevertheless, I persevered partly out of reverence for the history of British Manufacturing and the still-great name this company had. He (the MD) felt he had tried everything over the last 12 years: delayering, cost then budget centres, focused business units, cutbacks, TQM, recruiting competitors' 'stars', through to joint ventures on the Pacific Rim, and a supply-chain review with some competitive benchmarking that culminated in Business Process Re-engineering.

Ultimately, I made my presentation to the MD. He was a busy man but gave me two hours. Characteristically, he took the initiative and asked what else was there left for him to do? I began by pointing to a laminated A1-size wallchart of the organization's structure and, putting a red overhead pen into his hand, asked him to circle those parts of the organization making a loss. He circled the engineering manufacturing units. I asked him to take a blue pen and indicate those units which made a profit. He put the blue pen down and waved at the rest of the structure. I asked him what the rest actually did. It turned out that they sold engineering expertise in the form of consultancy to make products, and sold intellectual patents for products to manufacturers who made them themselves. I then asked him whether he had watched John Harvey-Jones' first *Troubleshooter* series on BBC. He had, and particularly remembered the Morgan cars episode. I asked him why the Morgan family had stonewalled and resisted JHJ throughout the episode. He assumed that it was NIH (not-invented-here) syndrome. I put it to him that the real problem was that JHJ had not understood what it was that Morgan was selling – he and his audience had not understood what the *real* product was. That JHJ imposed his manufacturing mindset onto making more cars, faster, to make more money was a result of his not understanding the product, which was not the Morgan car, but the *idea* of the car within the mind of the consumer and the feelings and complex associations about personal identity that the car triggered. This idea was so powerful that it eclipsed the need to actually have the car when you wanted it. People were prepared to wait, and in fact the waiting had become an indistinguishable component within the structure of the product itself, a component which could only be devalued through a traditional marketing approach to what was perceived as a niche product that was essentially, virtual.

I suggested that we left the room, and walk around the manufacturing site. The MD agreed: 'OK, but how does this apply to me and my business?' I indicated the wallchart. 'At one time,' I told him, gesturing at the manufacturing area, 'your competitive knowledge lay in the ability to design, configure, manufacture and deliver these unique products. Over time, the third world has invested in the engineering capability that was once an asset but which now has become public domain; similarly, you admit that 80% of the value of the product is outsourced, in fact your biggest activity is managing this supply chain. The truly competitive knowledge now exists in the heads of your people away from the shop floor. Your real work is being done on the electronic systems which define the products which you sell to other people who want to make them, and in manipulating your customer and supply-chain relationships. Much of your product is no longer unique, it would be cheaper to build overspecified sub-assemblies and reduce the level of customization. The future lies in developing expertise and selling ideas to partners in new markets – what you sneeringly call consultancy. The basis of your strength was always intellectual, it just got confused with actually making things yourself, which you cannot do and still make a profit.' We stared at the large empty sheds together.

I was lucky, I didn't own the problem, I could stand outside and see it. He couldn't accept that running the factory and keeping it busy was irrelevant. Two weeks later, I found a discarded four-day old *Financial Times* on a train and read that he had been replaced and a cost-cutting MD appointed.

Ultimately, knowledge management is interesting but needs to be balanced. Management as a term suggests a static resource where the key activity is capture, storage and allocation, which delights those who like to run factories, and made the tacit-to-explicit knowledge model so attractive.

Whatever knowledge we have is like a fruit. Without a customer, it is useless. But if we find a customer and it is not usable, it is worthless. The knowledge we create is the product of understanding patterns and their timing to create value. This means that knowledge management needs to be constantly redefined through knowledge development. In other words, we need to start talking about knowledge work being the product of *both* knowledge management (the square wheel that tends to dig itself into a rut) and knowledge development (the circular wheel that keeps running away from the square wheel). In the diagram, knowledge development is shown as a round wheel, connected by a 'learning bungee' that drags the square wheel forward into the future

SECTION

2

and redefines the existing knowledge that is worth managing, allowing us to discard those things we don't want to manage and introduce the new forms of competitive knowledge.

*Knowledge Management*: Managing what we know about what we do (static)

*Knowledge Development*: Creating new forms of knowledge for future opportunities (dynamic, redefines useful knowledge within a changing context)

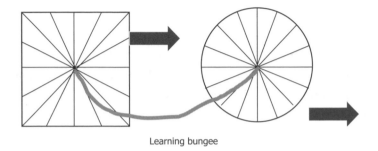

Learning bungee

There is a saying about coming to terms with unavoidable change. We can be told to wake up and smell the coffee. The knowledge whose time may have come may have a different aroma and accompanying taste. It's in our interest to keep it fresh.

## Implications

1 Where is the real knowledge in your organization that is worth keeping and developing now? A clue is to work out where you are competing: on price or on value?
2 Pay attention to knowledge transitions. What was the basis of your competitive knowledge? What is it now? And what is it likely to be in the future?
3 How long have you actually got before someone destroys the value of your existing knowledge?
4 Balance the effort you commit to managing knowledge with the effort you make to develop new, replacement knowledge.

## 2.2

# Golden Mantra

Knowledge work has become muddled by the convergence of IT, the learning organization and lean production thinking. I believe that unless individuals working in knowledge begin and end with the development of knowledge leadership, all they can do is optimize.

Seven years ago I was leading a lean production implementation process within a European automotive plant and something strange happened. I had always known that there was something profoundly wrong with lean production and certain types of technology transfer partnership, and that was not just because the books on the topic were expensive and heavy. The specific event that helped to make sense of my unease came after much discussion and criticism of prototype mission statements. I managed to summarize the underlying logic of the enterprise as this: if we can continue to cut the costs of production in the assembly of our partner's product, then we can expect the replacement products to migrate into our plant. This seemed to be a good thing.

The second linked experience occurred in the United States when I was facilitating a strategy workshop, and the issue of costs of production was being discussed. As in the automotive plant, the theme of margins, utilization, efficiency and continuous improvement reappeared. Casting my cynical eye over the performance target figures for the next 18 months, I posed the question of whether it was going to be possible to take out 40% of the cost of production in that period. This led to a flurry of confusion from the corporate board: Why 40%? Where had this figure come from?

The third experience occurred in a Business Process Reengineering conference at Cranfield University's School of Management. At the end of the second day of presentations I was stunned to realize that all the speaker case studies involved the redesign or optimization of what could only be called administrative procedures. The irony was that no one seemed to be interested in redesigning innovating processes that led to innovative products. The mindset seemed to be that innovation was purely about taking cost out of a process or informating the process to accelerate it and to make it smarter.

Now, putting it all together there seemed to be some consistent patterns or themes. A fundamental question that all enterprises need to ask themselves is, 'What are we actually selling?' In the automotive plant, we were consuming the ideology of lean production (which although frequently disguised, is based around the fundamental issue of the cost and timing of money and pushing the cost of borrowing down to the bottom of the supply chain). In order to sell capacity, we were selling a commodity that had to get cheaper every day. The more efficient we became, the less able we were to develop our own innovative products: we could only become prisoners of the process, wearing increasingly heavier chains. In the US corporation, the problem was that the existing technology of production could not be mined for sufficient cost reduction to deliver the investment necessary for a new replacement technology to provide value or cost leadership.

Indeed, deeper investigations showed that the costs of improvement were in some key cases outweighing the reported reductions in process costs, as what had been visible costs migrated into other areas. The Business Process Re-engineering conference made it clear that although its proponents used the language of innovating, they were really selling the optimization of processes to sell commodities, which over time can only be a disguise for slow suicide.

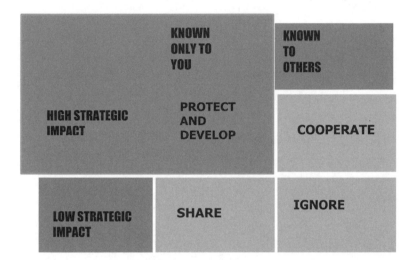

SECTION

2

In conclusion, it is clear that knowledge leadership is a prerequisite for survival. If an organization loses the ability to create new knowledge to deliver market leadership, it declines into selling commodities. The fundamental CEO knowledge leadership question or *golden mantra*, must remain: 'What do only we know, that has the potential for high strategic impact?' The supplemental questions that follow include: 'What are we doing to protect and develop this knowledge?'; 'How ready are we to exploit it?'; 'Where does it sit within our risk and reward framework?'; and 'How long have we got before someone copies or reverse-engineers our idea and commoditizes it?'

The sad thing is that all too often the initial CEO knowledge leadership question is met with a stunned silence. Once these questions are understood and answered, a supplemental logic applies that delivers a chain of timely, successive ideas to market within a competitive context that recognizes at least three forms of competition: with partners, who might perceive your logic before you do; with fast-emulators, who have the ability to commoditize your high-value transactions; and ultimately with yourself, in managing the obsolescence of your own transactions.

## Implications

1 CEOs' primary directive is to drive the development and delivery of knowledge leadership. From now on, CEOs must focus on proprietary products and processes.

2 Selling a commodity can be dangerous, but it can become the basis for changing the nature of the transaction into one where the basic commodity is differentiated by the new knowledge that can be wrapped around it.

3 It is essential either to recognize when to abandon the means of production as having no useful efficiencies to exploit or, at an earlier point, to know when to shift from continuous to discontinuous improvement strategies to mine deeper margins for investment in a replacement technology.

4 Putting 2 and 3 together can mean reversing outsourcing strategies by selling or even giving the means of production to the customer, and transforming the organization into a consultancy that sells its process knowledge without the costs of plant maintenance.

## 2.3

# Homes, Not Pyramids

The earliest stage of knowledge management was bedevilled by the idea that whoever knew the most, could manage the most 'knowledge' and run off with the glittering prize of the Global Knowledge Economy. In time, the futility of this exercise was glimpsed but the promise of better search engines, individual disciplines and meta-data tagging suggested that this was still attractive, and so the knowledge-farmers and their friends the knowledge-miners continued the trend. Dared they consider the possibility that the knowledge revolution was not going to be a computerized improvement on stamp-collecting or librarianship? No.

The literature of change and religious cults is littered with the accidental rubbish of ambiguous, key quotes and sayings that were crafted to mean one thing, and ended up being interpreted quite differently. When TQM (Total Quality Management) ruled the world, a key aspirational saying was: 'right first time'. This originally meant that if you plan it right, it will work when you want it to. What it ended up meaning was: don't build and test prototypes. This became a source of much amusement in Japanese companies.

The injunction of knowledge gurus to share knowledge has had similar unintended effects that need to be understood and resolved in order to develop sensible knowledge strategies.

SECTION

2

## Problem 1: Implicit economic paradigm

The economics of supply and demand apply to knowledge. Knowledge in the public domain assumes a low value and begins to look like a commodity, whilst that which is exclusive and personalized gains value. This probably explains the traditional confusion of knowledge with power and why many books about knowledge management contain very little actual knowledge.

The currency of the knowledge economy is ideas and their exploitation. What is largely missing in the emergent debate on how to configure organizations to compete in the knowledge economy is the application of economics to ideas and knowledge.

One of the key lessons of the Soviet experiment in nationalized economics was that in its heyday, 3% of privately-farmed land produced 84% of the edible food. Those things which were shared were run incompetently and were seen to have low value. The irony is that commentators are unwittingly suggesting the equivalent of state economics be applied to the exploitation of knowledge. If everything is shared, it will be perceived to have low or insignificant value. This has been obvious to anyone brought up in institutional housing, or who worked within a nationalized industry and watched it die.

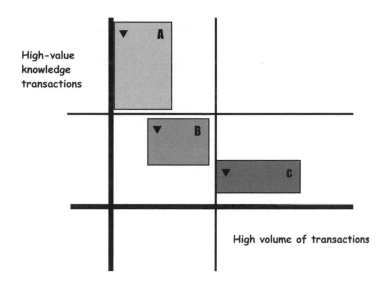

SECTION

2

The figure above represents a graph mapping the relative positions of the knowledge within an organization in terms of the relative value of individual knowledge transactions and their volume. Box A represents a healthy collection of high-value but low-volume knowledge transactions. These are delivered by creative individuals and are in transition between idea and prototype model. They are sold at a high daily rate, and have not been packaged. Box B represents medium-value knowledge transactions at a medium volume of delivery, delivered by trained consultants and with access to their methodology controlled by agreement. It is only a matter of time before the knowledge in box B slides into the area of Box C. Box C contains low-value transactions and hopefully these are delivered at a high volume, probably via a secure portal with low levels of interaction. The contents of Box C are designed for immediate customer use. The figure is an ideal. Ideally an organization would be in command of the timing of the declining value of its knowledge. At no point would it deliberately choose to position all its knowledge onto the market or continue to supply knowledge transactions where it was no longer economic.

**SECTION**

**2**

### Problem 2: Purpose and context

So I share this 'knowledge' of mine with you. How can you tell whether it's any good? How can you tell whether it really is knowledge, or information or even just structured data? How can you tell it's mine? And how can I share something with you, if I do not know what has value in your eyes and if we do not share the same purpose?

One of the commonplace experiences of knowledge work consulting is the request to advise an organization on how to establish a knowledge-sharing culture. This can go many ways. You can either begin trying to shift the culture by inventing or documenting stories that carry the knowledge-sharing-is-good message. It may be possible to cut to the chase, and point out that until the organization has a market value strategy that explicitly identifies the kinds of knowledge that need to be created, and plans their market value lifecycles, they will be largely wasting their time.

To put it another way. If you ever get confused about knowledge, try this. Firmly grasp the arms or underside of your chair. Take a deep breath, close your eyes and repeat the phrase: 'competitive advantage' to yourself until you feel better. Unless you can link your business strategy to the maintenance of existing knowledge and development of new knowledge, you can only waste time sharing things that need to be constantly interpreted and which may have only slight value. Remember; some facilitators use the phrase 'thank you for sharing that' when what they really want you to do is to shut up.

### Problem 3: Understanding the psychology of knowledge transactions

While the phenomenon of sharing experience has been researched, its psychology has tended to be taken as a given. There is consistent evidence that knowledge is shared among functional specialists in disparate organizations, and that it involves explicit trading in attributable ideas. The ability of individuals in specialist fields to retain complex relationships of knowledge attribution is known, but tends to be ignored. And yet the clues are there in successful communities of practice whose existence is determined by a shared, overarching sense of purpose. People will only share with those whom they respect and from whom they can expect a return or who share the same problem of preserving or reinventing identity. No one will share knowledge (something that has high potential value) with an idiot or a fool. The sad reality is that these high-value knowledge trades tend to occur across separate organizations and not internally.

The explicit psychology of these transactions involves:

- recognition (they are asking me this question);
- respect (they think I know something they don't);
- attribution (you can use it as long as you say where you got it from);
- reciprocal credit (I will answer on the implicit understanding that you will give me an equivalent transaction in the future); and
- shared perception of value (we both know this knowledge has real potential value if exploited).

## Problem 4: Language and knowledge worker

Is everyone going to be in a position to share knowledge? It's largely an intellectual and creative activity carried out by the same elite constituting the Human Capital within organizations that Scandia's original Intellectual Capital was designed to measure.

Let's approach the language problem, bit by bit. What is meant by knowledge? The failure to be explicit about terms like knowledge means you're going to get a lot of rubbish and expensive rework activity. A key question is: knowledge about what, to do what? After all, one person's knowledge might well be another person's structured data, or information. If we work backwards there may be some clues as to how to progress. If we tried to embed *data-sharing* into everyday work, we would do it by identifying outcomes and success criteria and work back to the necessary processes and activities that need to be managed, then define the performance data necessary to make a decision. If we extend the question to embedding information-sharing, nominated individuals would arrange the data into structures and review it within a time-frame to capture the emergent pattern or information.

Now we can attempt to answer the key questions: are we in control of our process, is it about to do something unusual, do we need to make a decision to either stop, start something new, or continue? If we step up the hierarchy: what would embedding knowledge-sharing into everyday work involve? It would involve bringing a number of information patterns together to create new cause and effect relationships within existing and new markets that offer the potential either to differentiate existing commodity products by wrapping them in the new knowledge or to offer completely new market values by applying existing information patterns to new contexts. In other words: combining different items of knowledge to change the rules of the game.

The truth is that knowledge work is not democratic, we are not all going to be knowledge workers. Not everyone is going to be either predisposed or equipped to create, far less share, any real knowledge in a world which still confuses data with information. The solution lies in creatively reframing the problem from knowledge-sharing into knowledge-building. If we ask people to build pyramids out of their own knowledge, this is going to be difficult because we must convince them to construct something that they are unlikely to be able to inhabit themselves – we all know that it's only mummies who get to stay inside pyramids. But if we ask people to construct houses that they can all live in, we are likely to build worthwhile homes. If we work on defining the type of knowledge we want to build, we can then focus attention and resources and start working on the problem of how to engage the right constituents in building it and making it happen.

## Implications

1  Reduce the number of idiots in the organization to the bare minimum necessary. No one will share anything with an idiot.
2  Employ the tactic of using language with real meaning. Deliberately stop talking about knowledge sharing; it only confuses people with its altruism and its implicit democratic message. Start defining aspirational knowledge frameworks within which new knowledge can be built that meets the need of delivering competitive advantage.
3  Create crises to focus knowledge contribution from those who can contribute, and remove investment from the aimless sharing of everything.

SECTION

2

2.4

# Rule of Three

Several years ago I was working with a newly appointed CEO who had been headhunted to turn around an engineering business within 18 months. It turned out to be a learning experience for both of us.

This CEO had been recruited on the basis of having managed an organizational shift from a functional to a process structure. (At the time, this was the prevailing managerial fad for disguising downsizing or staff reduction.) It became clear to me that he had never done it before. In my role as management coach, I took him aside and he cheerfully admitted that it hadn't been difficult to market himself as appropriately qualified to the headhunters, and that he had always been a good at interviews and playing the assessment centre game. As a result of our mutual candour, we decided to work together, sharing our experience to save the business, and in the process, I developed some useful elements of CEO knowledge from our partnership.

My first piece of advice was modelled on Montgomery's 'rule of three' (that if you identify the top three issues or goals and deal with them, then everything else will tend to sort itself out). We reduced business goals to just three and began to communicate these at the start and end of every meeting, but with characteristic flair he took it even further and began to personally communicate it with every employee and consultant. As a result of the focus on the top three goals, the corporate cultural benchmarking initiative was shut down as being an artificial form of work whose continuation could only distract everyone's attention from the three goals. This led to some interesting meetings and introduced a new level of risk in potentially masking useful data. This CEO told managers that he would listen to their reports only so long as they had a clear connection with delivering the three goals. Once they lost that connection he warned that he would stop the meeting and ask them to leave. The same approach was taken with major consultancies who scented blood in the declining performance of the organization. Before they began their pitches, he prefaced their presentation with his top three, warned them, and would then conclude their presentation the moment their old sales pitch appeared. This was always done with great good humour. It led to fewer and dramatically shorter meetings. The CEO also did something new at a personal level that showed he really was serious. He invited everyone as individuals to develop business ideas to generate new profit centres from the extensive site and its facilities and promised to attribute all contributions by recording them formally and providing a simple proforma for getting it onto the agenda for exploitation.

One adventurous individual developed an idea and took it to market, developing a new business on-site in underutilized buildings that brought in a major chunk of profit that seriously impacted the first goal. This was done in spite of the individual's functional manager and director blocking the idea at the outset. The CEO asked this blue-collar intrapreneur what he wanted as reward, since new expenditure was restricted. Jokingly, the intrapreneur asked for a Range Rover.

SECTION

2

Now this was a business within a corporation that allocated company cars according to management levels, and cars were the overt cues for status within the organization. After a moment's hesitation, he handed over the keys to his own Range Rover. The impact of this action was dramatic and led to a major shift in behaviour.

The result was a flow of ideas, initiated throughout the business, that began the shift that turned the organization back into profit through developing activities that began by creatively 'sweating' those assets that had been underutilized, then refocused the 'core' activity and finally went on to create genuinely new businesses. A side-effect was the managed collapse of the functional structure the CEO had been recruited to replace, which is another story.

## Implications

1  MIS: Make It Simple (identify and only work on your rule of three).
2  MIR: Make It Real (connect your words with individuals' reality through explicit action).

# 2.5

# Shiplogic

After working for several years with CEOs in what might be called crisis or business recovery situations, I began to notice some patterns in the way they approached them that might be called a process. For instance, I noticed that upon being appointed they very quickly indicated that the actual position was far worse than they had been told and renegotiated their package!

The generic process that followed could be broken into four characteristic activities or phases that can be understood by using the metaphor of a sinking ship.

- *Stage 1: The ship is sinking fast.* This tends to involve cost-cutting, driven through the existing functional structure and tending to reinforce functional power: bale or man the pumps, then find the holes in the ship and make them smaller or block them.

- *Stage 2: The ship is sinking slowly.* This involves the CEO developing an awareness of value in the business. It means physically picking up the product and asking two questions: 'Why do customers choose to buy this product?' and 'How much does it really cost to make, sell and service it?' The resulting investigations lead to the emergence of Implementers working across functions and the redefinition of value and the processes that deliver it. The ship is moving but only some of the oars are meeting the water.

- *Stage 3: Let's go faster.* Let's rethink the way we do business or consider doing it differently. What unique knowledge or relationships exist and which activities could be outsourced or franchised? Is the future about exploiting existing data about relationships and wrapping new knowledge around our commodity products? Whose ideas can we steal or shift from a different context? This is like redesigning the ship to go faster with a smaller crew carrying a more precious product. Now Implementors are in the ascendant, Stabilizors who love functions and processes are in retreat, and Creators who can't help having ideas are sharing them in the business instead of keeping them to themselves. Let's connect all the oars to the water, maybe redesign them to be more effective or start using a propeller technology, instead.

- *Stage 4: Let's go somewhere new.* What business are we in, anyway? Understand the declining asset values and visualize the crunch-time cues and scenarios for dumping existing technologies and relationships based on price. Deliberately focus on creating new market value. This is the equivalent of selling the ship to the crew, buying an amphibious aircraft, or setting up a travel agency to manage other ships' capacity. Creators are spending work time doing skunkworks product development, instead of going on management development programmes; individuals are creating new products and services within the business. Implementors are commissioning prototypes, stealing external ideas, communicating internal Creator ideas in the form of prototypes that change the way the business runs itself. Implementors are also killing stable products and processes and outsourcing them to Stabilizor organizations who can manage the cost reduction curves that result from commoditization.

The scary thing about the speed of the global economy is that over the last four years Stages 1, 2 and 3 are having to be done concurrently. I remember one CEO in the process of moving out of Stage 2 and into Stage 3 musing to herself that perhaps she should have recruited outsiders from the start and just incentivized them to drive into Stage 3. She continued to be amazed at how quickly what appeared to be smart individuals became acclimatized and as 'useless as someone who had worked in the business for the last 20 years.' The alternative is sometimes to manage the equivalent of a Viking funeral in order to go straight to Stage 3. The speed of decision making within a global knowledge economy means that nowadays Stage 4 is in danger of being done to laggard organizations by a competitor entrant from another sector who has no market history, no cultural affinity and is not sentimental about your technologies or people.

There are, however, some useful principles for dealing with the stages of this crude generic model.

SECTION

2

## Implications

1 Logic is useful but emotion works best in a crisis.
2 The trick is to develop everyone's hunger to participate in changing things.
3 Only ever show people that aspect of the crisis that they can work on: never show all the crisis stages in all their potential uncertainty and pain.
4 Use progress through the stages (if you have time) to develop the Innovating Stereotypes of the Creators and Implementors and to marginalize the Stabilizors and their intellectual factories.
5 No crisis, no learning.

# 3

# Working with Knowledge

# 3.1

# Death by Examination

In the time of the Chinese emperors, entry to the Imperial Civil Service involved a competitive examination requiring candidates to write down everything they knew. It was not unknown for candidates to die of starvation before completing the exercise. I admit to using a shortened version of this exercise.

Participants' instructions include a time limit of 15 minutes, a request for legibility, and the requirement to assign an accurate market value to the knowledge documented. Participants respond to the exercise in two dramatically different ways: one half start writing frantically after some hesitation, and the remainder stare dazedly at the blank sheets in front of them. After five minutes, I usually ask workshop participants to look at what they have written and explain why the exercise is futile.

Answers include the obvious point that 15 minutes just isn't enough time to write down everything, and the futility of the exercise is demonstrated by the need to answer a list of key questions before any progress can be made, like:

1  What do we know about what?
2  Why are we doing this exercise?
3  Who wants to know?
4  Why should I share it with you?
5  What do you want to know about?
6  What problem does this exercise solve?
7  What happens to my knowledge when I have finished documenting it, and who does it then belong to?
8  How can I assign a value to my knowledge without having a customer who has a sense of its value?

The exercise is useful in being both ambiguous and memorable, but also because it clarifies that knowledge has to be defined by value, ownership, purpose and context. In other words, we need to be clear about what we want to do with our knowledge.

A workshop participant challenged me to provide a piece of knowledge that had high value, that I had originated, and which could help her be more effective at managing change in her own organization. After demanding an up-front fee, my offering was to say that I knew that 'all change management initiatives die within nine months' (Newman's second law). When questioned as to the usefulness of this information, I pointed out the opportunity that it offers. If it is true (and I believe it is) then I have a knowledge opportunity to do two things: in the role of implementor I can begin planning its successor or repackaging within three months of starting; and as a participant, I need to jump ship before it becomes unfashionable, and align myself with its replacement.

In the case of the candidates for the Chinese Imperial Civil Service, their inability to ask questions that would enable them to connect their knowledge to a context where it had purpose meant they had no sense of the potential value of any of their knowledge. As Kent Greenes said: 'Make sure your knowledge has a customer.' In the change management context, if we work with the nine-month cycle, we can see the pattern, and manage our timing to create personal value by choosing to act to exploit the opportunity.

The next time you get into a black taxi-cab in London, ask the driver about 'The Knowledge'. What you will learn is fascinating. Essentially, 'The Knowledge' is the ability to recall the 400 routes across London which mean that you can get into a black cab and not have to carry your own London A–Z to direct the driver. If you have time, ask the driver about how they manage to learn and recall these routes and you will learn how individuals use different contexts to build their own complex mental maps, like the cab-driver whose interest in footballers meant he based his mental map on public houses and clubs they drank in, and another whose interest in musicology allowed him to structure his mental map around buildings connected with famous musicians and composers. However, does 'The Knowledge' represent the kind of knowledge we are interested in? Can we learn something about the kind of knowledge necessary to deliver knowledge leadership with the potential to make our business profitable? The answer is going to have to be no. 'The Knowledge' has a purpose and context for value, but, since its ownership is shared, it does not guarantee that the driver will make a profit.

Let's take another related example: the North-West Ambulance Trust. In 1997, this ambulance trust featured on a Radio 4 business programme as being unusual in the way it managed itself. You might think that the trust had applied knowledge of its route structures within the North West of England to optimize its response timings. This would only be a partial answer and would not really differentiate this service.

One simple way of defining the knowledge opportunity within a business is to ask CEOs what keeps them awake at night or what knowledge matters most to their business. And then you begin to see your opportunity.

SECTION

3

What kind of knowledge are we interested in? Think back to the nine-month rule, and the Chinese Imperial Civil Service candidates, and what is common is that the knowledge we are interested in is like fruit: it is probably defined by pattern, timing and value. The value of fruit depends upon the relative availability of similar fruits and is absolutely dependent upon the timing of the customer's hunger coinciding with the fruit's pattern of ripening. If we return to the black cab, the key to the driver's profitability lies, not in 'The Knowledge' of the 400 routes, but in the knowledge of where to be, at what time, to harvest the most profitable journeys. This knowledge remains fairly tacit and is not shared by cab-drivers. What the North-West Ambulance Trust did was to create a new form of knowledge by analysing call-outs over previous years to look for patterns in timings, locations, and types of injuries to create a predictive schedule for pre-locating ambulances and paramedics before incidents occurred, to deliver a service with new value.

So what is the knowledge opportunity? The knowledge opportunity lies in creating new forms of knowledge that deliver new value in the marketplace, by a process of asking questions about value and by understanding the patterns or information in the data within our own context. The most fundamental pattern within our shared context is the nature and the pace of the commoditization process at work in the global knowledge economy. Commoditization can force us to compete on price. Organizations within supply-chain relationships know that they are involved in a time-based pattern of exploitation which will ultimately destroy their ability to create new value through discontinuity, by means of destroying their ability to innovate. It is only a matter of time; the pattern is clear. A good way of communicating this pattern and its timing is to ask CEOs in supply-chain relationships to visualize the context within which they might have to give up their new Jaguar or Mercedes for a Volvo 740. The consequences of not creating new forms of knowledge which deliver new market values because of getting trapped in someone else's pattern and timing can concentrate the mind wonderfully. And as in most forms of rehabilitation, the first, most difficult, step is to admit the extent to which

SECTION

3

you have made yourself a victim, to identify the patterns in your own behaviour that made it easy, and only then to visualize a new, desirable context to move into, and the strategies to get you there.

## Implications

1  The knowledge opportunity exists when a piece of knowledge can be located within a context of purpose and ownership, doing something with the potential to deliver new value.
2  Everything becomes commoditized eventually. It is your job to create new forms of knowledge to stay ahead of this process.
3  Compete on value, not on price.

SECTION

3

## 3.2

# Goodbye to Knowledge Management

The problem with knowledge management begins with two words: knowledge and management. Just what do the words knowledge and management mean? And what do they mean when we put them together? The moment a consultant, academic or politician tells you that the meaning of a particular word or phrase doesn't matter, that is the moment to begin to take very special care of everything that follows if you want to survive.

This special care is necessary since the trend for IT professionals to rebadge old IT products as knowledge management technologies was never disguised, and it was sad to see the commoditization of an idea before it was ever really understood. But there can be no doubt that knowledge management has suffered from 'fadification' and has already followed the traditional cycle of enthusiasm, conferences, through to despair and ultimately the final indignity of inclusion within government publications.

Let's just explore 'knowledge'. The problems with the word 'knowledge' have different levels of difficulty. Here are at least two. The first level of difficulty begins with its inclusivity: it includes a broad range of terms like data, data structures, myths, intelligence, rumours, and even information. The second level of difficulty relates to the act of 'knowing', which implies that knowledge is defined by awareness; in other words, what you are aware of is what you know.

These levels of difficulty were compounded by the accidental combination of Lew Platt of Hewlett-Packard's famous saying, 'If HP knew what HP knows' with Nonaka and Takeuchi's linguistic confusion that led to the false dichotomy of tacit and explicit knowledge, and the awareness that downsizing in corporations had destroyed functional expertise. All that remained was for consultants to misuse Francis Bacon's 'knowledge is power' quote and the whole knowledge revolution took a major wrong turning and started to capture personal expertise in the form of documented processes, making this expertise available via intranets. The problem was that much of this 'knowledge' (what some people know) was about processes that delivered commodities whose market price was in decline. The appeal of this 'knowledge' management revolution for many lay in its apparent similarity with lean manufacturing. This linkage meant salesmen didn't need to learn anything new – old IT products and lean mass manufacturing concepts could be wrapped in the old, misunderstood learning organization packaging and rebranded with new knowledge management associations.

The clues to the future of knowledge work lie in the experiences of Shell and BP at the end of the 1990s. Their investment in managing a mistaken form of 'knowledge' did not prevent major layoffs and financial crises. And thus the definition of 'knowledge' begins to become clearer; it is probably not usefully connected with processes for delivering commodities, or even stable processes.

The problem with the word 'management' is compounded by its associations: that knowledge could be managed, that it was a matter

SECTION

3

of managing a discrete resource where the paradigm is one of storage, conservation and logical deployment. It was interesting that in both CEO Knowledge Visualization workshops I ran in 1998, participants all strongly questioned the usefulness of the term 'knowledge management'.

It has also been interesting to chair conferences to find organizations who deliberately don't use the term and who appear to be successful or, at any rate, profitable as a result. It seems as though the associations of the term 'knowledge management' actually make success more difficult to achieve. The emphasis on knowledge management is bedevilled by false associations with computers and databases. The computer is just a means to an end and not an end in itself. Building on de Bono's suggestion that the purpose of thinking is to remove the need to think, then perhaps the problem with the prevailing paradigm surrounding knowledge management lies in the way it tends to comfort its users by removing the need to think about doing anything new.

## Implications

1 Working with knowledge requires the thinking of new thoughts, and knowing when old knowledge has become the problem.
2 Managing knowledge about your existing processes, products and relationships must be balanced by creating new forms of knowledge that lead to innovating and the introduction of discontinuities.
3 What is seen as knowledge management will be increasingly outsourced whilst knowledge *development* is becoming the core competence for the enterprise.

# 3.3

# The Knowledge Idiots

One of the most depressing aspects of the knowledge revolution is the problem of language. As Ludwig Wittgenstein, one of the most successful philosopher/comics of the early twentieth century, put it: 'language is a cloak for meaning' and 'the limits of my language are the limits of my world'. Both observations capture the potential for inadvertent linguistic misdirection from two key words: information and knowledge.

The linguistic problem is the product of confusing the transaction or process with the word itself. In other words, we confuse the content of that which is communicated when we are informed, with information itself. Just because we are informed of something, there is still a lot of work to be done before we have any information. My early years as a remedial TQM consultant demonstrated this problem, again and again. Being a remedial TQM consultant was a wonderful experience because your client organizations already hated TQM because it had to have failed twice before you arrived to sort it out. There were three rules: first, try not to use consultant-speak, and find the problem they wanted to work on, and use that exercise to develop a learning process within the organization through JIT (Just-In-Time) demonstrations of appropriate tools.

A typical event at the beginning of such an assignment was to ask to see business performance information. This usually led to a presentation involving standard software packages of business data presented as information in the form of pie charts, bar charts, histograms, etc. I would ask for some information, and if that didn't work, ask what the structured data meant. The confused director would gesture vaguely at the diagrams and say, 'There you are, it's all there.' I would ask again, 'What does it mean? What does it tell you?' Wincing in confusion, the Director would say, 'It's a pie chart.' I would ask again, 'But what is it telling you?' The answer would come back, 'That dimension is bigger than the other one.' The third time this happened, I realized that something was consistently going wrong. Intelligent managers believed that the process of collecting and structuring data and representing data through software packages actually *created* information. What they didn't understand was that managing the data around transactions and structuring it did not create any information – all it did was to structure it. The act of translating that structured data into a pattern that had meaning still remained to be done. They were confusing an industrial routine with an intellectual act and the computer and the software conspired to reinforce this confusion.

The second example of this linguistic confusion of a transaction or process with the word itself can be seen in the way the word knowledge is used. And as with information, we tend to confuse the content of that which is known to us, with knowledge itself. At this point the knowledge issue becomes identified with the problem of defining consciousness – what it is, and how it works. This leads us nowhere, since even the experts tend to use analogies and metaphors to explain their philosophical and physics-based theories. The only other alternative at this point is to accept the knowledge issue as being largely one of how to structure all known data, in other words: the province of librarians. At this point you are probably feeling very bored indeed and would like an excuse to get your coat and leave.

This confusion is nowhere more poignantly illustrated than in the Enigma codebreaking story retold in a *Station X: The Codebreakers of Bletchley Park*.[1] A prevailing assumption of the graduates of Bletchley Park was that once we could read the coded Nazi wireless messages, we must win the war. In other words, once we were 'informed', then we had access to information, and thus it was easy to win the war. What was not understood was that the transcripts were merely recorded transactions. They had no meaning in themselves. In fact, if they were not quickly analysed and turned into information, then they had no value at all. Thus a Bletchley Park codebreaking veteran criticized Montgomery for not immediately finishing off the Germans in North Africa when he had access to the decoded Axis transcripts. Again, they could not see that all they had done was merely the first step in creating information and that what remained was to put that data into context, to empathize with the German Staff planners, understand their drivers, political pressures and constraints, and visualize the emergent pattern of their strategy to create some potential information that could be exploited. Oh yes – and run the British Army as well. The problem was to see the pattern by creating information and then to create some knowledge by putting that information into a context that could create some real advantage and stay alive, at the same time as being told by politicians to attack – with inferior technology that was a product of their pre-war defence cuts.

It is ironic that Turing's industrialization of codebreaking in the form of the innovative Colossus machine, with its ability to use optical character recognition to process code at 60 mph, made the information and knowledge problem even more difficult by swamping intelligence organizations with new volumes of content that needed interpretation.

SECTION

3

## Implications

1 Having been informed about something doesn't mean you have any information, and knowing something doesn't mean you have any knowledge.
2 Always ask yourself: what does it mean and how can I use it to deliver competitive advantage? What the codebreakers could not understand was that their decoded communications had to be transformed into information, and that information in turn had to be turned into something that could be used to win the war.
3 If you read a book about knowledge that doesn't make this distinction, then handle all the content with care.

**SECTION**

**3**

## Note

1 Michael Smith, *Station X: The Codebreakers of Bletchley Park*, Channel 4 Books, 1998.

## 3.4

# Knowledge is Not Power

As trained riot policemen know, there's nothing more dangerous than an urban crowd chanting nonsense. There is an informal rule of thumb for dealing with crowds and planning to contain their violence. First calculate the average IQ of the crowd and then divide it by the number of participants and only then do you have some insight into its volatility and potential for taking up a meaningless chant without considered reflection.

A great crowd of commentators on knowledge management are still carelessly chanting that knowledge is power without attempting to understand the kind of power involved.

Implicitly, the knowledge they are talking about is largely personal, often tacit and not codified or accessible. This power is the power of experts to deny or to delay, a negative power of subtraction or denial.

It says that if I hide this knowledge, then only I can make the decision. Sometimes this negative power is conscious, but, as is often the case with experts, they really don't know what they don't know and they don't know themselves what they have the potential to know, until you ask them a new question.

If we apply Goldratt's theories to organizational and process knowledge, the power of tacit knowledge to deny potential power becomes clearer. The great learning point of his book *The Goal* was that no process can go faster than its slowest bottleneck. In other words, the real power of individuals with Expert Knowledge Power lies in their ability to slow the business process down and not to help it succeed. This was the real reason behind the pursuit of the flat organizational structure; it meant that all knowledge was commoditized, all work could be done by anyone or at least learnt relatively quickly. The flat organizational structure was designed for a world without experts or for organizations with the ability to outsource their strategic knowledge. Hierarchies show you where the bottlenecks are in your process, where your decisions are made and whether your knowledge has been commoditized.

So, let's explore Personal Power in its organizational context. All you have to do is to establish yourself as the only person within an organization able to make key decisions. But how? By identifying key strategic processes at the heart of the organization and deliberately working to locate yourself at the heart of that process, you can become powerful. You gain power by positioning yourself in a bottleneck. You gain power by introducing inefficiency. And that should be an interesting thought for managers. OK, so you're going to establish yourself as a 'key' controlling figure. By virtue of what you appear to know, you are going to make yourself indispensable. A simple idea, yes. But bringing it about is difficult. It requires working all hours in order to prevent anyone else understanding the basis of your power. However, if you are indispensable, your weekends are vulnerable and you can't go on holiday because you have to be eternally vigilant at gatekeeping your bottleneck to exclude potential imitators and competitors. You have to keep a constant guard against anyone usurping your position. There are those already within the organization who might be learning enough to take your place. There are those outside the organization who might already have your knowledge. And there will always be those who actually want to destroy your positional power itself by removing the bottleneck entirely. You have to be alert to these people. They will try to make your tacit expertise explicit. They think it can be recorded. Once this is done, they will try to trace the patterns within it and convert it into a transparent process that can be shared. And sharing means your absolute power is diluted, the bottleneck widened, and Expert Power will be no more. As Harry Houdini discovered, balancing your effort in protecting your knowledge power has to be balanced by the effort of creating new knowledge, and new knowledge power.

The other side of the coin is the realization that the pace of innovation is determined by the speed at which your Knowledge Princes can create new knowledge and give it away. This speed of innovation is influenced by their boredom threshold for applying the same knowledge, their ability to identify and develop new users and to turn their personal knowledge into a technology and embed it into the work process. Until they have done it a few times, they will not develop confidence in their ability to donate and create something better. Many believe that the only knowledge they have ever created is their one and only child, and it will have no brothers or sisters to keep it company. Organizations are much like Machiavelli's fifteenth century Italy. The Knowledge Princes take the high ground within organizations to build their castles and use their position on trading routes (internal processes that cross the organization) to tax the movement of knowledge from source to market place. Sometimes they allow the Knowledge Merchants to stay, they entertain and feed them. Occasionally they imprison or torture the Knowledge Merchants, sometimes they rob them, but their knowledge is always taxed one way or another. The Knowledge Princes know that the longer knowledge can be delayed, the higher the final price paid by the internal customer. Machiavelli's *The Prince* is worth considering, if only for the fact that he wrote it in an attempt to get back into a

SECTION

3

position of power, and failed. Ironically, his knowledge of itself could not become power for him.

Another celebrated example turning out not to be powerful, is the sad story of William Smith and his 1815 geological map of England, Wales and part of Scotland.[1] Smith had the ability to create a new form of knowledge – geology – and construct his map using colour coding upon a two-dimensional surface to answer the question of whether there were valuable minerals under the soil. And yet he did not know how to turn that knowledge into power and suffered for it.

So is knowledge really power? If it were true, then we could reverse the phrase and equally logically say that power is knowledge. At this point, the chant becomes questionable. Obviously power isn't just knowledge, power takes many forms. So maybe knowledge is merely *a* power, and not power itself. When you explore the conditions necessary for knowledge to be powerful, or to be expressed in terms of action or events, then it makes some sense to note that knowledge has to be surrounded by significant prerequisites to be expressed as a power. It might be possible to express Power as the combined effect of having the appropriate Knowledge plus the ability to apply that Knowledge and an appropriate Knowledge Context within which to apply it. An alternative equation is to express Power as the product of the interactions of Knowledge and Marketing. Where Marketing is facilitated by the combination of Positioning, Sequencing, Perception of Crisis and Timing. What I mean by Positioning is the form that the knowledge itself takes and the way it is expressed so that it is recognizable as a solution to its audience. The Sequencing of knowledge is the structuring of the knowledge into a sequential flow of items that make up the knowledge, and their release into its community of users so that each item has a cumulative and logical effect, containing the seeds of the next piece of the pattern. Perception of Crisis is also key to the effect that makes power possible. It is only when Positioning and Sequencing are combined with a Perception of Crisis that it can be recognized as functional and its use made inevitable. Obviously, timing can be cold, like revenge, or hot when its context is manipulated. To cut to the chase: the power of knowledge is determined largely by theatrical manipulation and accident, as any amateur magician knows. But the crude technology of 'spin' and media manipulation of events has demonstrated that it is better to have a plan for releasing and exploiting knowledge than to trust to good luck.

## Implications

1 If you have no hierarchy, then you have no worthwhile knowledge.
2 Knowledge is only part of the complete Power equation. There are other variables to consider.
3 Your pace of innovation is determined by your Knowledge Princes' ability to give their knowledge away and replace it with something better.

SECTION

3

## Note

1 Simon Winchester, *The Map that Changed the World – The Tale of William Smith and the Birth of a Science*, Viking, 2001.

# 3.5

# Trick or Treat?

There is a point beyond which a concept should not go, a point at which a metaphor or analogy is no longer useful and illustrative, but can actually become dangerous. Intellectual capital has reached just such a point. As a chair at knowledge management conferences, I have studiously enforced the three strikes metaphor rule for speakers: use more than three metaphors to illustrate an idea and I must ask the speaker to leave the stage. There is a risk in guru-speak of replaying the scene from *Monty Python and The Holy Grail* where the Arthurian villagers are persuaded by a series of false analogies that if the witch in question really does weigh as little or as much as a duck, then she must be a witch. At the heart of the intellectual capital idea, a powerful question is posed, that questions just how serious organizations really are about their stewardship and governance of the organization as a value-delivering organization. This question can become hidden by its illustrative model, the unpacking of which beyond a certain level solves no real purpose and can only distance investigators from the messy activities that actually lead to innovation and deliver new value. When we investigate intellectual capital, we have to consider that although it promises to be a treat, it may be more of an intellectual sleight-of-hand or trick.

Whilst not the first to write on the topic of intellectual capital, Thomas Stewart's influential book: *Intellectual Capital – The New Wealth of Organizations*[1] built up interest in businesses and consultancies flirting with knowledge management, who desperately needed an explicit means of connecting knowledge management to value creation instead of simply presenting it as a hip thing to do. Stewart said some interesting things about intellectual capital, defining it as the sum of everything everybody in a company knew that gave it a competitive advantage. What followed was a cunning mixture of the wacky and the obvious, to the effect that:

1  knowledge and those assets that create and distribute knowledge can be managed just like physical assets, and
2  if knowledge is the source of wealth, then the goal is to invest in those assets that 'produce and process' knowledge (in order to become wealthy).

Intellectual capital tends to ignore the first proposition, preferring to develop thinking about these knowledge assets and ways of thinking about their management to create, deploy and mobilize knowledge that ultimately creates value in the market. The point is made that modern knowledge-based organizations tend to have low Net Fixed Asset (NFA) to Gross Market Value (GMV) ratios. In other words, if you calculate the GMV of an organization by multiplying the number of shares sold by the present share value, the aggregate turns out to be a massive figure in GMV. If you then calculated the NFA or, as it later became, the Replacement Value (RV) of existing fixed assets (originally what you might get if you sold your physical assets in a fire

SECTION

3

sale, but later, how much it would cost to buy new) and set it against the GMV figure, the lower the ratio, the more likely it seemed that this was an organization that lived, died and differentiated itself through having a significant knowledge or intellectual capital balance once the NFA/RV asset had been removed from the GMV total. In 1996, it appeared that the relative NFA/RV:GMV ratios for IBM and Microsoft were as low as 23.5% and 1.5%. The logic is clear: successful knowledge-based organizations are only interested in owning assets that create and deliver proprietary and differentiated knowledge.

But all that glisters may not be gold. For instance, would $100 in 1996 really have bought $23.50 of IBM and 93 cents of Microsoft's physical assets and $76.50 and $99.07 of intellectual capital? If we put ourselves into the investors' shoes, what do they imagine they are buying that approximates to this intellectual capital balance?

The answer is complex. First, they are betting on the organization's ability to do what it did last year again in the near future. But does GMV accurately reflect value? One only has to remember friends who were dot-com millionaires who were unable to realize the value of their shares because the moment they sold, the price would dip significantly. GMV reflects the high value of pension funds chasing limited investment opportunities. The fund managers have to go somewhere and they make the best of what may be a limited choice. Share price and GMV is a snapshot value indicator that informs the market on the latest state of betting on performance, as well as the limited investment opportunities open to investors. Similarly, the share value can be inflated because investors have no wish to sell their investment to recoup losses elsewhere. Microsoft lost $9 billion in GMV in 1999 because shareholders had to sell Microsoft shares to deal with massive losses in Russian investments. Share buy-back strategies can also artificially lift share values.

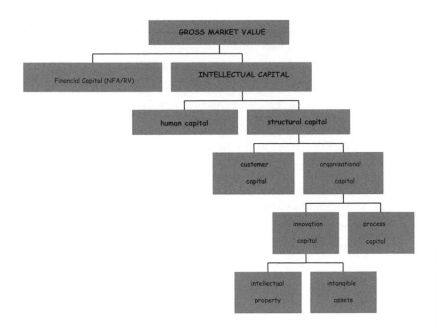

SECTION

3

Unpacking the intellectual capital balance leads to a consideration of at least three types of capital: human, structural and customer. Customer capital approximates to customer goodwill and brand value. Next comes structural or process capital, the value of the infrastructure and processes that are unique or differentiated from the competition. What remains last, and often the most significant proportion of the intellectual capital balance, is human capital, in other words, the potential value of the aggregated capabilities of individuals to create and renew market value. So it comes down to people at last, and the question alluded to at the outset is: if this value is significant, can you demonstrate that you are literally taking care of your knowledge business in a way that makes sense to you, your people and your shareholders?

I am not going to unpack this useful model further, but there are some observations that need to be made about the overall intellectual capital model and the way it attempts to decompose further into additional causal categories where structural capital not only includes customer capital but unpacks into organizational capital, which splits into innovation capital (with intellectual property and intangible assets) and process capital.

The mindset for this model remains academic and retrospective. Intellectual capital is the product of content rather than process thinking (it focuses on categorizing observations into classes within the model rather than trying to understand how and why they occur). Its primary weakness lies in the assertion that knowledge and those assets that create and distribute knowledge can be managed just like physical assets, and that decomposing the intellectual capital balance into discrete categories helps to solve the problem. It doesn't and it cannot. Businesses are not intellectual factories where success is determined by the size of the relative investment in one of these categories. All businesses are looking for the missing 'success cause and effect model' for focusing investment in time and money. Whilst the intellectual capital idea is useful, it does not connect with the need to understand how to manage an innovating ecology, or how to work with creative people to create discontinuous, new market value. This is not it.

With all that said, I have found it useful on at least three occasions: a hospital which started to manage its intellectual property as an asset; an aeronautical engineering business which realized that its human capital was largely contained in the heads of four individuals who went fishing together on weekends and were likely to retire at the same time; and, finally, intellectual capital persuaded a company to set up a formal innovating process to grow its intellectual capital and exploit it.

## Implications

1 Academic ideas tend to solve academic problems.
2 Concepts are two-faced, both trick and treat with both an open and a hidden nature; whilst they may offer new perspectives, they will also distort the thing being viewed.
3 Human Capital indicates the *potential* value of the interactions between your Creators, Implementors and Stabilizors. Invest in understanding and maximizing those interactions and you may create something that significantly grows your market value. Make it so.

## Note

1 Thomas A. Stewart, *Intellectual Capital – The New Wealth of Organizations*, Nicholas Brealey, 1998.

SECTION

3

# 3.6

# The Bridge

One of the problems of chairing knowledge management conferences and seminars is that if you are conscientious, you are forced to pay attention to the content of your speakers' presentations. The reason this may be a problem is due to my own obstinacy. I believe that not only should a good chair be able to introduce the speaker and their presentation, but as well as handling questions from the floor, the chair should be able to review all the presentations at the end of each day to summarize and reinforce messages, identify contradictions and spot the gaps that remain to be explored.

This is my self-inflicted penance. The reason why I do it, is that I know that I have a human tendency to listen to those things I like and ignore the rest. The issue of paying attention is core to knowledge management. A few years ago I was asked to facilitate an international consortium working on a major project. I found that the project leader, whilst understanding the level of risk involved, was unwilling to explore the risk and take appropriate action. I tried to persuade the project leader to undertake an exercise of visualizing failure, to plan the speech of apology to the joint board, the investors and the media and then identify why such a failure might have occurred and learn from it. The team refused to do it, justifying their choice through saying that exploring failure might make it happen. They weren't willing to experience the pain of simulating failure, exploring their discomfort and learning from it. I resigned from the project, and within 11 months the consortium closed down their investment.

Taking the role of conference chair forces me to balance my own tendency not to listen. But why should these presentations be so irritating? The reasons lie in the repetitious and confessional nature of much of the content.

Whilst I used to say that knowledge management was the victim of the three lost tribes of Information Technology (that failed to deliver any information), Lean Production (that published such fat books) and the Learning Organization (that failed to learn anything new since the early 1980s), I began to realize that the discipline of listening and summarizing the content of knowledge management presentations at conferences was teaching me something new, that there are only two types of knowledge management project: first, what we might call information management, and second, project management. And then I realized the obvious: that all projects are really knowledge management projects. All projects require a willingness to pay attention to process to deliver the specified outcomes. The project process is a potential framework for combining what has been learnt by the individual and the organization in the past, and it should also the product of deliberate explorative learning through anticipating the future, emergent risks. Project management exists in tension between the past and the future, it is about visualizing, constructing and walking across a bridge between what has been learnt and what might have to be learnt. It is this tension between the management of what we know and what we might learn that means that all projects are about

SECTION

3

the management of knowledge, what we choose to do with what we know, and how we plan to manage our ignorance.

Back in the halcyon days of Business Process Re-engineering (do you remember BPR?), an old statistic or urban consultant myth concerning project failure re-emerged from its original TQM source, to the end that: '70% of change projects fail.' And this seemed to be true of BPR toward the end of its fad-curve. But why should this be true and what does it seem to be telling us? As part of a research programme into BPR prerequisites at Cranfield University, we decided to interview people involved in major BPR projects to ask them whether their project had failed, and surprisingly, the results seemed to reinforce the myth: most interviewees felt that their projects had failed. But when we decided to go further and interview them all at the 18 months from project start stage, and asked why they felt that their project had failed, it was found that, on reflection, they felt that failure was down to two major reasons. First, that failure was retrospective. In other words, it was only after about 18 months that the organizations attempting to implement these major projects realized that their original vision had been unrealistic. This lack of realism had two sources: they had bought the consultants' sales hype and they had assumed that they knew more than they actually did. In the event, they ultimately discovered that they were themselves being used as prototypes to train their consultants! The second source of unrealism was that they wanted to buy transformational change without having to experience the pain of conducting the operation themselves. At the 18-month stage, they were able to look back and see this for themselves. The 'failure' they had in common tells us much about the way change was being managed as a project, and the way that only unrealistic aspirations could motivate organizations to undertake the risk. We are all wiser, now. Or are we? As Tom Stewart of *Fortune* said at the 2001 TFPL global CKO conference near Dublin, the real goal of knowledge management is an end to organizations purchasing Three-Letter Acronym change packages. What was common to all the BPR failure research interviews was the realization that something had been learnt that could not have been learnt otherwise.

The challenge today is slightly different. The new challenge is to manage the knowledge around delivering a project in such a way that it embodies what has been learnt from previous projects and anticipates what might be learnt in the process of getting to the goal.

## Implications

1  All projects are knowledge management projects.
2  It is only by exploring our areas of discomfort that we can learn to manage risk and pay attention.
3  Major projects require a process for managing knowledge about what has been learnt and what might have to be learnt.

SECTION

3

---

## 3.7

# Moments of Truth

---

Mutinies can be moments of truth. Having led a few mutinies, I know that no one is more surprised than the mutineers at the way they behave. Faced with a situation that you feel is no longer acceptable, the choice is either to refuse to participate or to surf the situation and your emotions by defining and declaring what it is that you really want. I led a mutiny in 1998, half way through a two-day conference on intranets. The problem with the presentations was that company speakers seemed to be more interested in selling their organization than in helping us to learn about intranets and their implementation. This was not necessarily their fault, it was merely that the organizers hadn't anticipated their audience's maturity or their questions. The fundamental nature of these questions led me to deploy a team of postgraduates on the Knowledge Management and Innovation option at Cranfield to pilot the development of an intranet benchmarking methodology. Five organizations, including a utility, an airline, a pharmaceutical, an electronic manufacturer and an oil company participated in this exercise.

Of course, there were other motives apart from the mutiny. One motive for the exercise was the commonplace IT consultant 'urban' myth of being invited to explain intranets to customers who made lots of notes and then proceeded to implement the idea for themselves. Eighteen months later, the same customer would contact the consultant to complain that it didn't seem to be working and could they help?

It seems to be easier to buy intranet technology than to make it useful to the organization. Although some would say that intra/extranet communication is a fundamental business structure, there is very little shared understanding of how to develop it so that it becomes the basis of doing business and delivers definite advantage.

With both these points in mind, a lifecycle approach to developing an intranet benchmarking methodology was developed with an ongoing consideration of business benefit throughout the intranet lifecycle. The outcome of the pilot was a new methodology for understanding a technology that is increasingly perceived as a prerequisite business architecture. In other words, it appears to some that you have to have it in order to play, and not necessarily even to approach winning status. Unfortunately, whilst intranet technology is being sold like a commodity, its successful implementation remains problematical. The research's initial outcomes were:

SECTION

3

1 *Without a vision, the people must perish.* The assumption is that intranets are an everyday business commodity. Buying an intranet is just part of the process that needs to start with identifying and visualizing the compelling business vision that forces individuals to rethink work so that the technology makes sense to everyone and is discretely connected to profitability.

2 *The business benefit planning Catch-22.* If we don't create a business case before we implement, then we won't have the basis for meas-

uring its contribution to performance, and we won't be prepared to change the way we behave and work to make it happen.

3 *Blind dog tends to bite blind man.* The blind dog will probably tend to bite the blind man whom it expects to lead it. Similarly, it is important to involve end-users in configuration, operation and domain ownership or take the consequences.

4 *Perhaps more of a financial drain than useful business plumbing!* Although data and information-sharing via an intranet has become a commonplace feature, it has yet to be established as a business-critical factor in delivering new and added value.

5 *Communication is not the same as sharing.* People use the words communication and sharing interchangeably. We can share anywhere as long as we know what others are interested in. Sharing is not bound by the intranet, in fact other technologies may be more appropriate like the coffee machine, lunching and learning, and smokers' corner! (There is a story that smokers tell, to the effect that they have better meetings outside the main meeting because their addiction is a bond that defeats hierarchy.)

6 *Electronic paper sends the wrong media messages.* The use of intranets as a means of electronic publishing reinforces the impression that the intranet is a command and control medium involving conscripts, and not about dialogue and creativity, and involving volunteers. Similarly, the two-dimensional nature of its web page format misses out on a potential three-dimensional, business model structure that is largely visual and closer to a business process model.

7 *Hit rates tell you nothing.* Site hit rates don't answer real questions like who visited, who got what out of it, and whether it led to new value creation or a better decision. We need a better diagnostic that links business process performance to intranet design and, ultimately, its performance.

8 *Possession doesn't necessarily confer advantage.* I was asked the question: 'Will having an intranet make me rich?'. I had to admit that it could actually make things a lot worse unless it served a real purpose.

## Implications

1 Information technology can be a differentiator as well as an accelerator of business activity.
2 IT tends to become a commodity faster than we realize and there can be no substitute for having products and services that customers really want.
3 You are not the only crazy person in the room. Listening to your heart and leading mutinies against assumptions can be very helpful. You also get to make some good friends.

SECTION

3

# Post-it, Cruel Partner, Aspirin and Alien

After a few years of working in the area of information technology and business strategy, some major points are becoming clearer.

We remain extraordinarily naïve about technology. As an implementation psychologist I tend to talk about at least four forms of technology: the Post-it, the cruel partner, the aspirin, and the Alien. Everyone approaches their next encounter with a technology with what I would call Post-it expectations. Post-it technology is benign, easy to use and requires no specialized teaching, it is quickly understood, uses existing abilities to model relationships and can be as sophisticated as we wish it to be. This is what Windows promised and what excited Steve Jobs at that first Xerox demonstration of what ultimately became Windows technology in December 1979.

People actually want technology to be like Post-its but they often end up with a 'cruel partner' technology, where the relationship starts out well with a brief but intense flirtation, leading to a consuming passion. But after a period of time, one has to work much harder and give much more in order to maintain the relationship and replicate the high. After a while you may find that you have given up nearly everything for a relationship with a technology you are not sure works any more, because you have to keep changing yourself to make it useful.

The third technology analogy is the aspirin. Aspirin is a homeopathic remedy which works on the idea that if you have got a headache, your body exaggerates that discomfort to kick-start the body's immune system to release endorphins from the brain to swamp it. Like the aspirin, you buy the technology because you are ill and you can implement this technology to divert attention from the real problems. But the business can still fail because it did not address the real cause of sickness.

The fourth technology analogy is the Alien. As in the film series, there is no negotiating with the Alien. In fact the Alien isn't really interested in us at all, it has its own agenda. We buy it because it suggests an abstract modernity, it offers a means of redefining our business and simplifying it. The problem is that although the Alien is intellectually exciting, it is cold, and tends to use us as a host for its children or eat us for dinner before moving onto the next victim.

We want the Post-it but what we actually get are variations on, or combinations of, aspirin, cruel partner or the Alien.

It is very difficult to sell what is loosely called information technology to clients in terms of providing new value. New value is something that purchasers tend to avoid because they don't understand it. You can only sell IT on the basis of commoditizing existing low-value, high-volume, low margin transactions. This is why the only e-business value proposition that actually stands up to any serious scrutiny is Business-to-Business, which is a cover for taking cost out of business processes or shifting the cost of borrowing down to the bottom of the supply chain; continuing the computerization of the old Business

SECTION

3

Process Re-engineering logic of redesigning what were essentially administrative processes.

The migration of technology value can tell you a lot about what organizations are actually learning about technology. For instance, intranets were sold on the fatuous basis of removing centralized publishing costs and delay. Consultants added up the visible costs of centralized publishing and demonstrated that by sacking those involved and making the medium electronic, a major saving could be made. The reality was that those centralized, visible publishing costs were in turn replaced by invisible, local costs which, because they were not monitored, did not exist. What was not considered were the issues of delegating editorial and document-disciplines down to those who already had busy jobs and were now being asked to do even more and as a result began to do their electronic publishing badly. It is now accepted that retrospective return on intranet evaluations are a significant waste of money, but they were a step in the right direction, which was toward the issue of value. What has been learnt through the Cranfield/Cap Gemini Intranet Benchmarking in 1999 and the Intranet Value research that followed, was: the common sense that said an intranet wouldn't make you rich by itself. An intranet is an environment and not a technology; it's how you interact with your transaction that delivers the value, and it's possible that an intranet could make things worse rather than better. This ultimately led to the decision to work on developing a Reverse Balanced Scorecard approach to planning intranet value, since if you don't involve the business in planning the value and only then consider the means of delivering it, you don't change behaviours, focus on outcomes, and you forget why you are doing it. The recent implementation of corporate knowledge portals seem to be repeating this experience. Whilst much of the e-business experience tends to show how technology is being used to differentiate commodities by association, and not necessarily as a means to that end, the jury is still out on whether WAP can create a genuinely new means of differentiating commodities. After all, Amazon is still selling books, it's not even commissioning new books by data-mining the contents of its customer transactions.

Ultimately, if your addiction is to technology you are in for a bumpy ride. If your addiction is the creation and delivery of value, you just might get what you want.

## Implications

1  Forget IT, try to understand technology.
2  Purchasers tend to project their expectations onto the technology they buy.
3  You are only as good as your addiction. So, what's it going to be?

SECTION

3

# 4

# The Organization vs. Knowledge Management

# 4.1

# The Blind Storyteller

In 1976, a book was published that enjoyed a brief notoriety at the Royal Military Academy at Sandhurst. The book was Norman Dixon's *On the Psychology of Military Incompetence*.[1] For a brief period, this book assumed the status of a minor pornographic masterpiece within the Academy: unofficially, it was read by everyone and it tended to fall open at the reader's favourite pages. The result, for me, has been an abiding interest in the psychology of management incompetence: an interest that is essential to any serious student of the topic of knowledge and its application. Dixon's book was heavily influenced by the post-Great War literature promoting the attractive myth of innocent volunteers cruelly massacred by incompetent generals. The problem with this myth was that it promoted the stereotyping of military leaders as incompetent purely because they were military leaders! This myth was double-edged: whilst it led to a generation of leaders like Montgomery who resisted political pressure from Churchill until he could fight the kinds of battle that he knew he could win whilst keeping the casualties down, it also led to a belief that the military option was itself immoral and a product of incompetent logic.

Years later, I was working as an internal consultant within a large organization and began to recognize that much of what I was observing every day within a civil, business corporation was contained within Dixon's book. We tend to forget that the professional British military have an advantage over civilian organizations: they get to bury their own dead and their mistakes themselves, and they get to do it in public. This is a very sobering and emotional learning experience: one that tends to promote serious reflection and a determination never to repeat that particular mistake. I began to wonder why, if the British military had such a tradition of learning from mistakes, Dixon hadn't changed his title to something more useful, like *The Psychology of Management (as opposed to purely Military) Incompetence*. Such a title would have had a much greater impact but would have been much harder to research. As a result, I have deliberately exploited the idea of studying management incompetence in the knowledge that it usefully provokes managers to rethink their behaviour and to review the myths of organization manufactured by universities, consultants and publishers. If we reflect on the volume of research literature including best practice that is manufactured and its minimal impact on management behaviour and performance, then the very futility of the research activity itself becomes interesting.

So let's imagine that there is a conspiracy, and instead of looking for the sniper on the grassy knoll or replaying amateur videos of alien dissections, let's play with the idea that a conspiracy to maintain management incompetence is alive and well, and explore how it might be working.

I began to question the prevailing research and publication paradigm after twice witnessing violent disagreements with published case studies from audiences who had actually participated in the events documented. In both cases they pointed out that the case

SECTION

4

studies simplified a complex situation and promoted a myth that the change process had been logical and under control. Mistakes were not mentioned, mistakes that had provided real learning to those involved but which could not be included within the official case study since it did not promote a myth of management competence. Needless to say, senior management had commissioned the academic researcher and sanctioned the interpretation, but how could the official account contradict actual experience?

In the days when I used to run Outdoor Management Develop-ment programmes, I was intrigued at the tendency of senior manag-ers to demonstrate groupthink: a form of constructive fantasy about their own motives, how they had approached things, and a tendency to focus blame onto outsiders to their group. This was such a repeti-tive feature of intact team behaviour on complex outdoor exercises, especially after a significant failure to complete a task, that I began to video and replay exercises to directly confront this tendency to recreate the recent past into a more convenient form. The problem is that at the very least, case study literature promotes a retrospective and dangerous storytelling myth of order and logic that reinforces stereotypical behaviours. Its second purpose is to promote positive brand associations around the subject of the case study, and as such is part of the war against the consumer and the serious investor. As a literary form, its key weakness is that in not including contradictory impressions, interpretations and points of view it assumes that the reader is an idiot.

SECTION

4

The irony is that apart from the first chapter, the content of serious books about change management are largely identical. All they can teach is programme project management. This 'knowledge' is only valuable to those who haven't done it before. And the longer the gap between change processes, the more incompetent managers become. In the absence of a significant literary heritage documenting business failure, managers are only likely to become more and more vulnerable through the case study method. The tendency to reconstruct business reality as a convenient myth can only ensure that eager MBAs will remain unable to recognize reality, even when it hits them.

A telecoms manager introduced me to his team, whose sole purpose was to monitor the internet for stories about their employer. He assured me that most of these stories on the internet were officially denied, but had a tendency to come true. As has been often said: if you don't understand your history, then you are doomed to repeat its mistakes. The promotion of myths can only promote incompetence. Choose your storyteller with care: their words may be attractive, but they may be blind.

## Implications

1  Measure the cost of incompetence, and invite everyone to participate in reducing it.
2  As well as documenting best practice, document incompetence.
3  Promote a blame culture: don't blame anybody, but promote working with real data and assigning real responsibility.

SECTION

4

## Note

1  Norman Dixon, *On the Psychology of Military Incompetence*, Pimlico, 1994 (originally published by Jonathan Cape, 1996).

## 4.2

# Simon Says: Don't Copy

I used to be surprised at the willingness of leading organizations to play host to benchmarking visits. After all, in order to maintain competitive advantage, it must be in the interests of organizations to hide their practices from public view for as long as possible. Gradually, I began to realize that it was not necessary to hide successful practice. I learned that the more you showed people, the more confused they would become. Just because you let organizations visit your business, it doesn't mean that they will readily understand your real basis of advantage.

But why should this be so?

First, there is the time delay factor. From the moment your advantage becomes apparent, is noticed and publicized, documented and analysed via a compliant academic or industrial sector association survey, through to receiving the first visit, the exemplar has at least 6–12 months to work on identifying and developing their next leading performance. In effect, once the visitors have seen it, it's already well on the way to becoming obsolete. So why not show it and build your brand at the same time?

The second advantage is your visitors' inability to see through to the heart of your strategy. In other words, there is a persistent tendency to only understand those symptoms or superficial aspects of your strategic thinking that are familiar, that are recognizable. But if the exemplar is intent on knowledge leadership – that is, developing a new form of knowledge and exploiting it to create new value in the market – then unless you are equally creative and ruthless, you will only recognize those parts of the strategy that are familiar. It is the unfamiliar that will make the difference and the unfamiliar is usually invisible. An associated issue is the tendency to ascribe your success to something that they feel their own organization has discarded.

We tend to forget that our prevailing tendency is to see pretty much what we want or expect to see, and that our ability to recognize situations is very much dependent upon our existing repertoire. We recognize those things that are familiar but we tend to exclude those features that are contradictory or threatening. It is very difficult to perceive the new or the novel. We tend to be trapped by our cognitive inheritance into only recognizing the familiar and reinforcing the primacy of our own specialisms. I first began to gain an inkling into this problem when I studied survival in extreme circumstances and began to notice the behaviour of hostages and schoolchildren. One of the distinctive features of hostages' behaviour is the 'Stockholm Syndrome', the tendency of captives to identify and take on the behaviours of their dominant captors. Another was the tendency of pupils to model the behaviours of teachers when their teaching method was defective: if you can't understand what teacher is doing, do the next best thing, behave like them.

Modelling or copying external behaviour is no substitute for having a knowledge strategy of your own. Benchmarking within your business context will diminish the gap with the exemplar but cannot deliver leadership. Working within a traditional approach to benchmarking, which is to model the exemplar's behaviour, is rather like marking time in today's economy. It could ultimately kill you by forcing you to compete on price.

There are, however, two alternative approaches to benchmarking which are difficult to sell but which offer advantage: Breakout Benchmarking and Fantasy Benchmarking.

Breakout Benchmarking works on the basis that someone, somewhere (outside of your existing business/technological context) has solved your problem: it's just that you don't know it. This involves two different activities: visiting organizations outside your sector and looking for things you can steal and apply within your own, and deliberately analysing your business processes and using metaphor to break out of your original context, solving the problem within that metaphorical context and then translating it back into your original context (as in the diagram below).

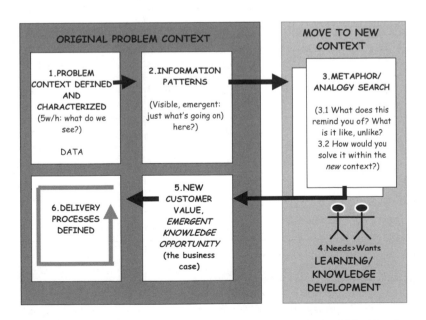

Fantasy Benchmarking involves at least two knowledge leadership visualization games: Predator and UFO. Predator requires visualizing the unexpected attack of an out-of-sector competitor without any legacy profile but with the ability to think clearly and surgically dismantle your business. UFO (Unidentified Flying Organization) involves visualizing an organization that does not exist but which you invent to benchmark against. The UFO is measured in new ways, does new things, laughs at your legacy logic and you have to catch up somehow.

## Implications

1  Understand your own tendency to see what you want to see, to focus on style and externals and miss the knowledge leadership at the heart of the exemplar you may be visiting. Let's face it; if you were even close, they wouldn't let you in.

2  Breakout Benchmarking: deliberately go scouting out of your sector, look for the organization that has already solved your problem and isn't threatened by you.

3  Fantasy Benchmarking: visualize the business that doesn't yet exist, the one whom it would be worth copying if it existed, the one that would create the crisis that would redefine your business and deliver knowledge leadership.

# 4.3

# The Elvis Trap

As a student of management incompetence, I have always been intrigued by the repetitive, commonplace statistic suggesting that 70% of systemic change implementations fail. I have done some retrospective research on this statistic and, combining it with my own experience, now interpret it in a slightly different way. I think what it tells us is potentially quite interesting. First, these systemic change implementations are usually consultancy-led, involving the sale of a packaged approach. Second, the client tends to confuse the consultant's selling process with strategic facilitation, which reinforces the need to purchase the package instead of focusing on the strategic context. Finally, when you talk to someone a year or 18 months into an implementation they tend to describe what they have endured as failure, because they have become educated by the change process to realize the naïvety of their initial expectations at the original point of purchase.

As a result, and as an implementation psychologist, I use simple creative techniques to overcome this 'happy shopper' syndrome and one of the most useful in the repertoire is reverse thinking. This is usually applied in at least two ways: to visualize completion and a wish to get there, and to visualize failure in order to prevent it happening. Few clients enjoy both processes. Some initially argue that exploring anticipated failure might actually bring it about. They probably also believe that being photographed will allow the photographer to steal their soul. However, some discussion on the meaning of their own behaviour in being scared of exploring failure often brings about a change of heart. What is interesting about this exercise is that the second or third anticipated cause of failure for an implementation always turns out to be that C-word: 'Culture'. After a while, I began to realize that there was something strange about the way we used this word. In organizational terms, I believe that its use or invocation *means that we have decided to fail* and in encouraging us to focus on externals we avoid the core issue, which is not the paraphernalia of culture and its measurement but the issue of work itself. The real issue that we face is that over a period of time, the competitive environment makes stable forms of work obsolete, and our problem lies in defining new forms of work and discarding those which are no longer sustainable.

One of the problems for HR directors lies in the historical accident of benchmarking as a technique for overcoming NIH (not invented here) mindsets, and the movement of sociologists like Rosabeth Moss Kanter and anthropologists into the management arena. The combination of the two created an artificial technology of culture that led HR into a new field of benchmarking successful cultures in the belief that by copying the external indicators of success, companies could become more competitive and modern. What I have found fascinating about companies dedicated to market leadership is that they have very little time to waste on this kind of exercise. If you are successful, you don't have time to waste on creating new forms of artificial work. You know exactly what you are doing, or at the very least it's

SECTION

4

too successful for you to consider its potential weaknesses. If you are failing, you probably don't understand why it is happening to you. This explains why leading organizations have always encouraged cultural benchmarking and visits from outsiders. They understood from the way that Japanese lean production was researched that you learn more about the researcher than the subject being explored. They knew that time dedicated to copying someone else's culture was time taken off from the real issue of how to compete in an increasingly global market, time that could have been better used in creating your own unique source of competition. This is not to suggest that the study of culture is a waste of time, just that it is not the real focus for success, merely the outward clothing disguising a time-based success formula.

Understanding an organization's culture requires an historical analysis of the way in which their technology has evolved. Unfortunately, most cultural studies ignore this invisible, historical problem-solving process that delivered their stable technology. Models and theories of organizational culture are like the dust-covers on desk-top computers. The shape of the dust-cover can only hint at the nature of the technology underneath. Without understanding the context and the processes that have culminated in a technology described by a cultural model, it is very difficult, if not impossible, to *copy* such a technology, since this involves a learning process that has to emulate the original crisis or opportunity that created that technology. Furthermore, the purchaser of cultural models cannot introduce these models unless they are prepared to symbolically divorce themselves from their old technologies. Unless a 'marriage' crisis occurs or adultery is committed, they remain in love or at least indifferent to new opportunities.

The problem with benchmarking what appears to be winning cultures is that it can only offer clues without creating the skills of implementation. It is like trying to become another Elvis by adopting his diet, sleeping in his bed and marrying Priscilla Presley. The literary success of Peters and Waterman's *In Search of Excellence* allowed them to introduce an artificial technology of imaginary emperors' suits, purveying style through a similarly redundant technology of

SECTION

4

imitation, the fashion for which survived even when the businesses they considered to be excellent collapsed.

## Implications

1 Understand that your culture is just a by-product of solving a succession of problems involved in stabilizing a technology and is not a technology in its own right.
2 Cultural benchmarking is no substitute for developing new forms of knowledge that give you leadership in the market.
3 If you become a market leader, your culture will not be an issue except for unscrupulous academics.

SECTION

4

## 4.4

# Curse of the

# Knowledge Princes

A few years ago, I was asked to design a time management course for delivery by internal trainers. What this actually meant, once I got through the rhetoric of the need to deliver authentic material and processes in a language that reflected the culture and style of the organization, was that the client was unwilling to spend money with existing vendors of these programmes whose visible by-product was a variation on a physical or electronic filofax. In other words, they wanted to pay for the product and not for the wrapping that it usually came in. Fair enough, I thought to myself, and so I set to work, gathering data and interviewing employees to define the real need for the programme and the type of local spin necessary to connect it with the everyday reality within that organization.

After two days of interviewing, I realized that I just could not continue working on the project. I met with the sponsoring board director and explained why this exercise had to stop. In effect, I had realized something was fundamentally wrong with the concept of time management as a product. It was like trying to win a war by only arming your soldiers with packs of Elastoplast. The message being sold by the phrase 'time management' is that individuals are incompetent because they don't know how to manage time properly. The reality, as I discovered, was that individuals can't manage their time because they don't know how to prioritize, and they don't know how to prioritize because they are in a mess. They are in a mess because no one has had the anger or intelligence to clarify and simplify the purpose of the business in a way that allows individuals not just to prioritize their everyday activities but also to say, 'no, I don't do that; and on reflection, there's no need to do that at all.' A key component of this mess is legacy work and the historical trail that it leaves behind. Individuals continue to do the work they can do in preference to the work that they should be doing because its novelty means they don't fully understand it, and so they avoid doing it, preferring to work on what they understand.

The business I was working for was in a mess. Exploring the internal confusion that was originally going to disappear through the consumption of time management training, I realized that there was an underlying assumption about how the business was won and done, and that this core assumption was the real source of the confusion. In other words, we're in a mess because we cannot tell the difference between what must be done and what could be done. The client was an engineering organization whose selling process was based on winning bids. The underlying assumption was that it would only ever win one in every ten bids, and so it had to prepare 200 bids in order to win 20. This had created a situation where employees could no longer differentiate between a speculative bid and a probable success. The resulting volume of detailed iterative work in preparing bids had led to some costly mistakes in winning bids that had been publicly embarrassing. Accordingly, I found myself and my team redesigning the bidding process and the accompanying documentation to deliver a virtually concurrent bid documentation process. Through an historical analysis of successful bids and core competencies, we shifted the business model assumptions from a 1:10 to a 1:3 hit rate based on identifying those opportunities that we could win.

The big shock for the directors was the realization that the fact that they were world-class experts in their field did not in itself prevent them from running their business badly. The financial crisis and loss of confidence meant that the directors began to understand that their technical knowledge was not as important in this case as being able to simplify and focus the business. This refocusing under crisis led to the identification of the Knowledge Princes within the organization – who presided over the decision-making bottlenecks – as being the real obstacle to clarity. Then came a programme of working with the Knowledge Princes to develop a knowledge succession plan that had two purposes: first, to widen the decision-making bottlenecks so that at least three individuals could be developed to make that key decision instead of just one; and second, to liberate the existing Knowledge Princes to start thinking about the shape of the emerging decisions that they would have to be able to make in the near future that would differentiate their products and services through applying new knowledge.

Ultimately, the business became more of an explicitly knowledge-based business when it shifted itself from doing everything in-house toward becoming in effect the manager of a supply chain, outsourcing all its commodity knowledge products and services.

Individual incompetence, like organizational incompetence, is often the product of a systemic failure to apply knowledge and the inability to recognize the nature of the emerging crisis.

SECTION

4

## Implications

1 If people act as though things are a mess, then they are a mess.
2 Teaching people to say 'No' is harder than you imagine.
3 The expert knowledge power that was the basis of your original business could become your worst obstacle to survival.

SECTION

4

# Bodybuilding for the Knowledge Organization

One of the problems for knowledge management is the suspicion with which it is viewed within organizations as the new kid on the block. Is knowledge management a fad, an art-form that just manages to state the obvious using confusing language, a discipline in its own right, or an alternative perspective for understanding organizations and the nature of competitiveness?

In organizations that have bitten and sometimes swallowed the knowledge management bullet, there is often a self-conscious deployment of fashionable knowledge management terms that seem to suggest modernity, but with very little accompanying evidence directly connecting the acquisition of this new language with any real change. The vendor use of knowledge management to repackage old IT products has increased this cynicism. The fact that investing in IT will not of itself lead to new productivity, or even new forms of work that create new value, means that serious thinking about IT and knowledge management budgets can often parallel the military logic of some First World War battles, where generals kept feeding more men into battles that were already lost, but which appeared to be winnable with the commitment of just another few thousand men. In both cases – war and IT – the issue is not about investment, faith or commitment, but the need to reconsider and integrate purpose and means.

The business may have been inoculated with knowledge management, and the language of academics and writers on the topic has been acquired, but what – if anything – has changed? Does this linguistic acquisition merely demonstrate a chameleon-like ability to simulate what appears to be the clothing of modernity without any fundamental shift in perception or mindset? The language of knowledge management needs to be complemented by a common perspective of actual and potential organizational knowledge transitions that demonstrates a shared understanding of the key knowledge that used to be (past), actually is (present) and probably will be (future) the basis of competitive advantage.

Knowledge doesn't become value without an internal process of realization and recognition. Let's examine the issue of knowing, believing and doing. I can smoke cigars and know that, ultimately, I will die of cancer if I don't stop. I won't believe it until I find it difficult to breathe. It is possibly then that knowledge will become belief, and only then that I will connect knowledge to my personal context, believe it, and then act. So someone else's knowledge will not become real to me until I can connect it to my personal context, and it may take some pain to make that connection real. Knowing stuff isn't enough; I have to make the connection that enables recognition. And only then am I likely to act.

If knowledge management isn't leading to my organization consciously managing the commoditization of its products and services, attempting to deploy the application of knowledge to innovate and differentiate, then it isn't working. This leads to the obvious realization that the employment of a CKO for longer than three years, is an admission of failure. Clearly, in these terms, the virus has failed to transform the system. The system has survived, and the virus has become a nominal hostage to the organization.

Let's briefly review the three Organizational Knowledge Imperatives that drive an internal knowledge economy.

First, how to manage the knowledge that's worth knowing? This means having the ability to have a knowledge plan that can ensure that the knowledge that is needed for everyday processes and innovation processes is consistently captured and built into a generic process structure that can be easily accessed by teams. It also means having the ability to identify the knowledge that is worth commoditizing and outsourcing.

Second, how to learn faster than the competition and embed the knowledge into appropriate media? This requires the ability to view the organization from outside the organizational box and by wearing the predator's shoes, to continually question the lifecycle of organizational knowledge, running premature visualization exercises and learning from them.

Third, how to create new forms of knowledge that deliver new market value? This means anticipating the boredom of the market and constantly visualizing something new and different that means you are in control of the market's attention span and perhaps, like MTV, determining the attention deficiency of a generation through the continual reduction of the duration of camera shots. This is about having a sequence of timely products that succeed and reinforce each other whilst anticipating their own redundancy, just as Intel used to be able to with its x86 chain of processor chips; leading the competition a merry and painful dance to the pulse of your own beat. And making sure that when the beat stops, you leave an uncomfortable chair open for your competition to sit upon.

The three Knowledge Imperatives require a keen focus on clarity within a context that is in continual transition. The two constants are the decaying value of applied knowledge and the realization that the acquisition of enabling technologies without visualizing their part in

SECTION

4

delivering new value, means that whilst the organization's physiology may grow, its psychology and perception remains fixed. We are still doing the equivalent of putting microchips into bows and arrows to measure the archer's pulling-power without enhancing target acquisition or automating delivery.

If knowledge management is to deliver, it needs to be the complementary mirror of the business strategy and, like IT, needs to be built into the perception and muscles of the organization, and not an extra competing function in disguise.

## Implications

Build knowledge muscles into the way work is done, by:

1 integrating your knowledge strategy into your business strategy, so that the connection is seamless;
2 ensuring your knowledge strategy answers all the questions within the three Knowledge Imperatives; and
3 reviewing your competitive knowledge in terms of what it was, is and will be, and also building explicit actions around knowledge and capability gaps.

SECTION

4

# 4.6

# The Naked Emperor's Wardrobe

Organizations that deliver successful market innovations tend to grow, and as they grow and spread their tentacles globally they face the problems of connectivity, engagement and performance that accrue from their new scale. Upon examination, this new scale can be more the duplication of a successful craft approach globally than a truly integrated business based on shared global disciplines. Success can promote an attitude that avoids analysis of the craft success formula, like the New Guinean tribesmen believing that the photographic process would steal their souls. In other words: if it ain't broke, don't try to understand it, just do it more. Successful innovating is an exciting and high-energy activity involving multidisciplinary teams from concept to market exploitation, manufacture and delivery. All too often, these teams are so exhausted when they reach key milestones, and relationships are so raw, that they are reluctant to dedicate themselves to additional shared time for thinking about learning. The pain is not something anyone wants to relive with strangers, because this means talking about failures and omissions which upon reflection should have been anticipated, and no one wants to talk about their own incompetence. So, if the naked emperor is successful, all he can leave his successors is an empty wardrobe filled with virtual clothing that cannot be worn.

But if they have a charismatic leader who can see beyond the team, and who is willing to push the issue, then some focused, high-energy facilitation can lead to documented lessons being captured, documented and ultimately implemented. The problem for innovating organizations with a scientific bias is that all too often the original source of their strength – their academic prowess – carries its own discrete curses. The academic curse includes the assumption that knowledge can only be managed within discrete specialist departments mimicking university departments and, just as worryingly, that documenting an item of learning and making it available means it has been learnt. The truth of the matter is that the university faculty/departmental structure for developing and applying knowledge is artificial and flawed, being originally based on clustering apprentices and priests around a great teacher. Another aspect of the inherited academic curse is that the difficulties and pains of integrating knowledge across specialist functions and negotiating the resulting crises to get to the delivery milestones become seen as the core cultural rite of passage, embodying the core experience of the organization. No pain becomes associated with no gain. In fact, no pain means you can't have done your job properly. So if you want to belong to the culture that created your boss, make sure that you leave no useful guidance for the next cohort, just like your boss did. And so it goes on.

How does it go? Those who can, do; those who can't, teach; those can't do either, research and write it up in the form of publishable papers. As I commented to the ESRC (Economic and Social Research Council) review of UK management research: we really don't need more management research, what we do need is to start implementing what we already know. But to deliver innovative products and services we need the doers – the researchers and the teachers – on the same team, working out of the shared context of the process that takes us from concept to market. And we need to work together because the costs of inadvertent reinvention are unsustainable, and the length of the product to market process, with handover at key milestones to the next team, offers many opportunities for collective amnesia and only partial recollection.

As I have said elsewhere, the best diagnostic for an organization's ability to manage its knowledge lies in examining its ability to apply existing and new knowledge to its projects, and integrate what its teams have learnt into everyday activity that destroys unnecessary duplication and enables creativity to be focused on developing knowledge that is truly new and usable for others. Unlike the organizational emperor satisfied with his nudity, we can design some real, flexible clothing for specific occasions that can fit everyone who needs to wear it.

Unfortunately, learning from real projects is defeated by the absence of:

SECTION

4

1  *A basic process model for locating what has already been learnt by individuals and teams.* Instead of steamrolling over existing experience, the valuable learning that has been previously gained should be captured, acknowledged and built into the teamworking and problem-solving model. Teams require a simple, top-level generic model within which individuals can locate new and useful information gained from reviews. A brown-paper model with generic key stages that is annotated by outgoing teams is a simple example. Useful knowledge about innovation doesn't exist in a vacuum. A drawing is more powerful as an aid to recall than a list. Even the learning of lists relies on the mind's ability to use visual images to aid recall and mentally store data and structures. We all need a basic, visual map to start from in order to learn. If we cannot locate what we have learnt within a visual model, we may never

be able to find it again and, more important, develop an awareness of just how much we *don't* know.

2 *Permission to customize learning within a generic process using authentic language connected with personal reality.* Invite learners to annotate the generic process to indicate where the learning has occurred and where it needs to be applied. The receiving team should check their interpretation of the lesson and use their own language to personalize learning and make it transferable.

3 *Helicopter (process) thinking.* This is the key ability to distance ourselves from the action, to stand back and understand where we are now in the process and where we ought to be going next, as well as which knowledge needs to be applied, and when. This type of thinking includes the willingness to control the use of creativity for variety as well as depth of ideas, and the sensitivity and the courage to say 'Stop!', just like the Special Air Service patrol commander in the Gulf War who recognized the impossibility of operating in their designated patrol area on disembarking, due to the complete lack of cover for concealment and courageously ordered his team back into the Chinook.

## Implications

1 Beware the academic knowledge model: it is unsustainable.
2 Build a generic problem-solving model that can be used globally with all teams, and encourage customization by individuals.
3 Develop process leadership behaviours that keep teams focused within their process.

## 4.7

# Who Needs Groundhog Day?

If we go back a few years, you may, like me, remember the story of BP and its lessons learnt. This was a good story, told by Kent Greenes, who went on to presumably better things outside BP. This story, recently re-told by Chris Collison, explained how BP had applied the US military's After Action Report methodology to their own pipeline and business operation to achieve significant improvements in performance. This success story was subsequently balanced by the caustic comment of a friend in the US military who asked the significant question: just how many lessons do you have to document to prevent lazy soldiers sleeping underneath armoured vehicles parked on marshy ground? Without wishing to raise the political agenda of just what is and is not common sense, his question is connected to the issue of record-ing lessons and their impact. Several international consultancies and their customers have made significant investments in databases for what they rather carelessly described as 'Lessons Learnt'. Several of these databases share a common history of high cost, a high volume of documented lessons, and very little objective evidence of application of these lessons, and a political need to pretend that the investment and the technology has worked. And just like government ministers, subsequent organizational reshuffles moved the guilty on to new opportunities and reduced any interest in forensic investigation and laying of blame. As I have said before: beware of those who call for a blame-free culture, they often have a guilty conscience to hide. There are at least two ironic observations that can be made at this point. First, that it is extremely rare that the custodians and servants of the lessons database actually apply the lesson-capture methodology to the way they do their own work. And second, that an unfortunate metric has evolved suggesting that the more lessons you have on your database, the better it is. Sadly, the complete opposite may be the case: perhaps the fewer lessons left on your database, the more effective your learning may turn out to be.

SECTION

4

I shall illustrate. It can be argued that the existence of a large number of these lessons may actually indicate a failure to deliver real lessons that are truly learnt. The point being that if these lessons remain in the database and are not specifically located within a business process, SOP, internal best practice for decision making, or role contract, then they remain lessons documented and not, in reality, lessons learnt. There is an old change management joke that applies to learning as well: how many consultants does it take to change a light-bulb? The answer is that the number of consultants is immaterial, the light-bulb itself has got to want to change. The problem for the idea of the learning organization remains that until individuals have seen a learning organization in action, they won't understand what it means or even want to change, and if they haven't modelled it in their own lives on a small scale, they will continue to think that a learning organization is one that aggregates a lot of learning in databases and makes it available or broadcasts it. Ask yourself: when do you know that an individual has learnt something? When their behaviour changes. The secret and dark history of lesson databases resembles that of the enthusiastic parent who bakes a fabulous party-cake with icing and candles, sets the table and forgets to invite any guests. Baking the cake is key, but there is a complementary need to invite the guests and probably to understand their reality in order to provide items that they can and will want to eat. As I have said before: if you want to understand how organizations manage their knowledge, look at the way they manage projects. If they don't capture the lessons and integrate them into their processes and behaviours, then they don't understand knowledge management.

There are two minor issues about lessons and learning: language and timing. The word 'lesson' is synonymous with punishment (we say 'They have learnt their lesson' when we have taken punitive measures) and mistakes ('They got it wrong, and have to learn their lesson'). It may be more useful to use a slightly different term instead: 'learnings'. Managing the timing of learnings needs to reflect what we learn from thinking about knowledge as a fruit whose value is determined by managing the timing of the hunger of its customers and its ripeness.

In too many organizations, including those with lesson-databases, life resembles the film *Groundhog Day*, where every day is largely identical but where those involved act as though each day is unique. Even where there is an explicit process for identifying and documenting processes, it can be the case that the team can provide over a hundred lessons with potential for application. This surfeit of riches can defeat the original purpose, since all lessons have the potential to reduce future risk: what do you dare to ignore?

What is needed is basically three things: first, to integrate learnings into everyday work so that they make a difference; second, to create a strategic pull-mechanism for new learnings to attract attention to building lessons that cumulatively make a difference to performance, and finally, a means of quickly transferring key learnings from teams taking innovative products and services to market, to the teams who are following in the track of the leading teams.

Learning integration is an additional activity to lesson documentation. It involves a form of learnings triage or sorting – What is the

SECTION

4

potential benefit of application? Whose lesson is it to apply? Where would it be best located? – integrating it into existing processes or media, and finally, measurement of benefit. This would need to be complemented by a strategic learning plan. Such a plan begins by focusing on strategic goals and identifying the knowledge or know-how gap in terms of existing practice and prioritizing clear know-how themes (what do we need to learn to know how to do to deliver the goals?). Finally, fast, tactical transference of learnings from leading teams to those following in their slipstream can have major benefits: a kind of learnings baton-passing, with all the benefits of being passed directly with the language of emotion, fresh from the battlefield by veterans to the new troops taking their places.

Ultimately, success could mean an empty learnings or lessons database.

## Implications

1  A lesson documented is not necessarily a lesson learnt.
2  Learning has occurred when behaviour has changed.
3  A learning system needs to connect learnings to strategic learning themes.

# 4.8

# Pain is the Spur

A consulting friend rang me up to ask my advice about his assignment to facilitate a senior management team. He was facing the perennial problem of the professional problem-solver: how to sell a solution to a problem that the client doesn't want to talk about because discussing it undermines their personal myth of competence and control. How do you sell a solution to a problem that politically cannot be discussed?

He complained that whenever he showed them 'modern' management thinking they groaned and accused him of introducing management jargon that needlessly alienated them and only served to distance them from a frank discussion of the real problems of the business. They kept asking him to translate his language into theirs. Of course, the senior management team had a point. But when I reflected on his complaint, I felt that there was an underlying message that he sensed, but hadn't articulated. What they were saying appeared to be: talk like us, use our words from our context, and we'll listen. But the deeper response to their charge of his use of an alien language of change was: actually we don't want to change, and we are imposing our own language on you to prevent any serious discussion of any change. The language of learning or change is usually expressed in terms of the solution. As professional implementors know, you usually don't know you have a problem until you have seen and understood the solution. As time went on, my consulting friend began to ask questions about his consulting predecessors in the organization, and some dusty files were produced.

To his great surprise, most of what he had thought of as being new language and models to the senior management team turned out to be language they were quite familiar with. Initially he thought that they were in denial regarding the need to change, and yet it was clear that what he was proposing to them was not new. What was going on? Why were they playing this strange language game? After further consideration it became clearer. It turned out that the senior management team were cynical about his problem-solving language because they were already familiar with it; they had heard it before, and nothing had happened. The problem was that although they were familiar with the language of change, they had never had to apply it. But never having had to apply the models and solutions, they had developed a form of change-cynicism out of their familiarity with the language of change and their ability to successfully sabotage it by demanding a translation.

So if you are trying to influence senior management in an organization, it is essential to understand how to go about influencing what can only be described as a learning process. So when do senior managers learn? Well, just like everybody else – when they have absolutely no alternative and survival means they have to consider developing a new identity to cope. Let me illustrate with some further examples.

There is an urban consulting myth that suggests that the recent explosion of corporate portal implementations was due to a series of articles about corporate portals in an inflight business publication tucked into the seat-pocket of first-class transatlantic seats. Once they had checked out the laminated emergency procedure flightcard, seen the inflight movie and browsed the duty-free brochure, all they had left was this business publication. And having nothing else to distract them in the lonely hours above the Atlantic Ocean and unable to sleep, they had time to read and inwardly digest.

A few years ago when I used to consult in lean production implementation, I commissioned one of my best researchers to interview successful lean production businesses about their motivation for adopting lean production as a way of doing business. As is often the case, the real reasons for adoption were quite simple and predictable. In spite of the hype surrounding lean production techniques, it became clear that organizations didn't adopt a lean production philosophy because they were interested in Japanese culture or because it was an intellectually stimulating idea. They did it because if they didn't do it, they were dead. This becomes even more obvious when you visit Japan and realize how limited the applications of lean production are outside specific industrial sectors and, even more interesting, how and where it has failed because of its limitations. Life becomes very interesting when there's no practical alternative to what is staring you in the face.

A recent piece of research suggests that the most significant management development or personal learning for senior managers occurs in situations when managers are asked to undertake the implementation of a new initiative that takes them out of their functional experience and into their zone of potential incompetence. The sheer sense of exposure heightens awareness of the need to take nothing for granted and think in terms of process instead of comfortable context. And it is only in exploring their own zone of incompetence, and living with the risk of deliberately moving outside it, that real learning occurs.

SECTION

4

## Implications

1 If necessity is the mother of learning and invention, then let's create situations where it has to occur: encourage staff to consider investing MBA fees in setting up their own businesses. They might actually learn something of value beyond a new technical language.
2 The cry of 'jargon' may mask the denial of the need to change or to learn.
3 Knowing or having heard about an idea cannot be compared to the knowledge to be gained from actually having made it happen and learnt from it.

SECTION

4

# 4.9

# Your Knowledge or Your Life

Every organization faces the problem of realizing the potential value of its knowledge. Whilst it may once have been true that if HP had known what HP knew it could have been much more profitable, the reality is that the productivity of knowledge is dependent upon two linked abilities: the ability to recognize the potentially high-value knowledge that can make the difference, and the ability to apply it. To have the one ability is useful; to have both is essential.

Research suggesting that the longevity of organizations with a lifespan of more than 40 years was due to a strong emphasis on overarching values has mistakenly led to businesses trying to force-fit statements of values into their organizations. At best this reinforces paternalism and at worst it treats employees as reluctant conscripts ordered to whitewash the company coal. What has been missed by such research is two alternative interpretations. First, that 40 years probably was the lifecycle of the value of the knowledge of the organizations studied. In other words, it took 40 years to optimize it and make it obsolete. The second conclusion is that businesses that lasted longer than 40 years had to make a shift in technologies. In other words, they had to manage the death of one piece of knowledge and the adolescence of another; and the articulation of values was the bridge that connected both forms of knowledge. While the values provided continuity, they were never a substitute for having another piece of high-value knowledge to exploit.

It is convenient to be cynical about the apparent failure of the virtual economy's spoilt children, the dot-coms, but the dot-com phenomenon has its own story that was easily obscured by its own roller-coaster hype and the vacuity of its writers' narratives. The apparently short lifecycle of the phenomenon demonstrates the speed at which a new piece of knowledge can be commoditized in the global knowledge economy. What took 40 years now takes two. The critics of the dot-coms failed to see the limitations of the digital economy; all it could do was to aggregate demand and take cost out of B2B (business-to-business) processes, taking JIT to its logical conclusion in pushing the cost of borrowing down to the bottom of the supply chain, onto those who could least afford it. What the digital economy could not do was to create genuinely new value. The internet demonstrated that what we had taught for too many years was not true: technology had shifted from being an enabler to becoming a differentiator of commodity products. But this was not enough. The digital economy has been a mechanism for commoditizing knowledge and not a means for creating new knowledge. When will Amazon commission new videos and books and deliver them online? Similarly, when will CRM in online banking be more than a disguise for the fact that the financial products being offered are just a commodity? The truth that every Morgan car owner knows is that if you have a product or service that is truly niche, then the more difficult you make it for the customer to acquire it, the greater the perceived value. The dot-com knowledge was itself commoditized before it could develop any new knowledge and in turn transform it into products with new market value.

If we think about the ability of an organization to apply a new piece of knowledge, this facility is subject to its own Catch-22, or circular, reinforcing logic. Many years ago one of my researchers rang me at home to tell me the good news about his investigation into the root causes of successful implementation. In great excitement, he said that he had discovered that bad companies had bad implementations. He paused for breath, and I anticipated his conclusion, that good companies had good implementations. He asked me how I had known what he was going to say. I replied that it was obvious, and that his mission was to explain what he meant by good and bad companies and good and bad implementations. It was obvious and yet underneath it lay a deeper truth that he managed to capture; that the 'good' companies in his survey were continuously rethinking their business, refocusing it; and that although there was a level of initiative fatigue, their business and project management skills were continuously flexed and developing. The 'bad' companies had infrequent implementations, and because of their lack of practice, they tended to fail.

The truth about an organization's ability to apply knowledge is that you are only as good as your last implementation, and if you don't practise, your ability to apply new knowledge will decay and disappear.

The key to an organization's success lies in its ability to redefine the productivity of its knowledge. This means being in control of its own knowledge lifecycle and the frequency with which it commoditizes and buries its old knowledge to replace it with new high-value knowledge. What this means is that organizations are always in two worlds: the worlds of the future and the past, simultaneously piecing together the fragments and traces of emergent new knowledge whilst at the same time being distracted and partly submerged in the workings of the old. We are either constantly redefining and connecting the new knowledge of our experts into new processes that reduce risk and deliver new value or trying to cut the cost of running old processes based on commodity knowledge that can be purchased anywhere.

SECTION

4

## Implications

1  The digital economy has accelerated the decay of knowledge.
2  An organization's productivity of knowledge depends on its ability to recognize high-value knowledge and apply it.
3  You are only as good as your last implementation.

SECTION

4

# 4.10

# The Dunce's Cap

It is time to be honest about the limitations and opportunities of the idea of the learning organization. When writers exhorted businesses to become learning organizations, what they were really talking about was the need to learn to practise paying attention systematically, in order to survive. Naturally, the idea became a consulting approach with a workshop methodology that rapidly became a commodity. Yet in its early days, it seemed to offer an escape from the successive, cyclical consumption of new Three-Letter-Acronym initiatives which, in turn, decayed into fads.

The idea of the learning organization is an analogy that is in productive tension with itself. Just as the Italians say that there is only one thing more dangerous than organized crime and that is crime that is disorganized, so it may also be true that there is only one thing more dangerous than a learning organization, and that is one that is conspicuously failing to learn. The tension sits between the keywords, learning and organization. The unwillingness to use this tension, to explore it creatively and with humour, can only continue to promote further confusion between the process and content of learning.

The learning organization became significant when the pace of innovation, driving increasingly abbreviated product value lifecycles within the knowledge economy, meant we needed a new paradigm. It provided a space within which to consider how to act which had the potential to be filled with knowledge about knowledge (or $K^2$) to fuel creative thinking. But the point I want to make is that a learning organization is not the sum of its parts. In other words, the appearance and substance of a learning organization is in the way it behaves and demonstrates learning and not in the content of the education that its individuals consume.

The idea of the learning organization has several fallacious connotations. First, the idea that an organization can learn, like an individual; second, that models of how individuals learn can usefully be extended to include organizations; third, that the consumption of learning is itself a good thing; and finally, that individual performance improves with the consumption of learning content. This confusion is exemplified in the old MBA question, 'when will I know everything?' and the soothing answer I always gave, which was 'soon, my child, soon.' And I had to give this answer because they had mortgaged their past to invest in an uncertain future. By investing in their MBA programme, they wanted value for money and, as in psychotherapy, they confused consumption with treatment, and reduced their anxiety about what they didn't know by trying to know even more. So the more MBA material consumed, they better they would be. The reality of the MBA could have been retitled: MBAFL (MBA as a Foreign Language). Of course you don't need to know or learn everything, what you really need is to be able to deploy business language within the correct context and develop the ability to ask better questions. So we don't necessarily need to learn more, we need to learn how to learn and unlearn, to be able to use appropriate business language, think independently and ask better questions.

Continuing in this vein, Sri Sridharan (then an Intel Fellow) pointed out to me a few years ago that he knew smoking big cigars would probably make him ill, but until he was actually unable to breathe, he wouldn't believe it. Knowing something is not the same as being able to do it. Major corporations have a tendency to confuse analysis and documentation with learning. Documenting failure is only one third of the necessary learning process. The confusion of content consumption with the learning process is exemplified in the idea of lifelong learning: that we need to go on learning as the world changes in order to participate. The idea is fine, but this means that individuals are being sold the idea that the consumption of university-driven content leads to more productive individuals. What has been forgotten is that it is the duty of academics to say only the obvious. If we go back to the environment in which the learning organization makes sense, we need to remember the truism that innovation is not necessarily a product of education. Highly educated people can usually tell you why something is impossible, where creators just go out and do it anyway. Education doesn't necessarily support innovation; rather, it has a tendency to stifle it through enforcing intellectual conformity.

So maybe we don't want learning organizations, maybe what we need is learning individuals who are easily bored, who have the ability to ask questions like: What's going on? Why are we doing this? How long have we got? What do we do next? Individuals and organizations are trapped within another cognitive contradiction: that we tend only to recognize problems for which we already have a solution. In other words, you don't know you have a problem until you see a new solution. Which means if we haven't got the repertoire, we can't see the problem. If we can only learn by solving problems, then the eternal problem of the organization has to do with identity and continuation of that identity. When we talk about the resistance of organizational cultures to change, what we need to understand is that culture is the by-product of solving a cycle of problems whose outcome is usually a technology. The inability to shift the culture means that

SECTION

4

the organization is unwilling to solve new problems; in fact, it is probably unable to see them at all and is unable to divorce itself from an obsolete technology. The eternal problem of the organization is: What kind of problem do we want to solve? What we do know about teams is that when they find themselves unable to solve a problem, they tend to redefine the problem into one that they actually can solve. Organizations are the same.

The learning organization is about continuously solving the problems of who we were, who we are and who we want to be. This involves learning to love the feel of the dunce's cap on our heads and enjoying the freedom of considering ourselves to be a lot less bright than the world takes us to be as an organization.

## Implications

1  Learning is done by individuals and groups within organizations, and not *by* organizations.
2  The individual's learning process is more important than the content of any educational programme.
3  Knowing is not the same as believing or having the ability to act and ask good questions.
4  Without a shared problem-solving language, individuals cannot work together to focus attention on solving the problems they have never seen before.

# Potemkin Cities

In all societies, the higher the status of an individual or social group, the more abstract and symbolic their language becomes. Accordingly, the greater the gap between a role and the action, the more virtual their form of work becomes. It can be argued that the real purpose of MBA education is to acquire business language, and that such education might be better handled by directly teaching it as foreign language that individuals aspire to speak, and thus by reciting the ceremonial prayers and putting on the clothing of business priesthood, they become licensed to practise.

In such a context, an essential piece of knowledge lies in being able to distinguish between substance and abstract symbols of high-caste language that are purely ceremonial. It is becoming increasingly difficult to make such distinctions in an increasingly virtual world where a type of abstract, symbolic behaviour and language, invested with moral and caste associations that was formerly the preserve of monarchs and bishops, is rather irritatingly becoming the norm for politicians and corporate business leaders.

It is very tempting, from their great height within organizations, for leaders to become prisoners of their courtiers, and to give in to the temptation to project their role through symbolic language and behaviour, and to extend this licence to their own courtiers. Hitler and Napoleon both gave in to this tendency with predictable results. It could be argued that France will never recover either from the symbolic language of national myth that Napoleon and de Gaulle both foisted on it.

A famous example of the deliberate use of the virtual is the apocryphal story of the Potemkin village, probably generated by jealous courtiers. Grigory Potemkin (1739–1791), perhaps the most loyal of Empress Catherine II of Russia's lovers, apparently spared neither men nor money in his abortive attempt to colonize and populate the Ukraine. The story goes that, not wishing to disillusion the Empress when she toured in 1778 and to disguise his failure, he assembled what appeared to be populated villages, but which were really painted canvas village facades with soldiers playing the parts of jolly peasants to be viewed from the Empress's barge. These 'villages' were then dismantled and relocated further downstream to reinforce the impression. Clearly there are real villages and there are Potemkin villages. The difference between them is that you cannot inhabit a virtual village indefinitely, especially when the weather changes. A virtual village can capture an aspiration, but it takes a lot work to create an approximate reality.

Organizations need aspirational language in order to make transitions that are essential to survival. These can include documents using terms such as: overarching goals, visions, purpose, strategy, values, objectives, mission, aims, etc. The danger in this language is when it fails to provide a realistic context for action. What distinguishes the language of corporate aspiration from a minimalist corporate Potemkin furniture that looks great in the catalogue but

SECTION

4

which you couldn't sit on – or from a call to arms? The question to ask yourself is whether we are viewing a real village or city, or merely the virtual symbols designed to create the illusion of corporate governance and reinforce a myth of leadership.

The psychology of implementation teaches us some hard lessons. The factors that contribute to corporate impotence include the following.

1 If you can't visualize the new, preferred state that you need to go to, then behaviour is unable to change enough to make it happen.
2 If you don't achieve congruence between ideal and individual behaviours, you don't get focus and you increase alienation.
3 If you can't answer the questions WIIFM (What's In It For Me?) and SWDIDN (So What Do I Do Now?), then people will assume that you're not serious, and that it's not worth putting effort into lining up with the message.
4 If you don't demonstrate purposiveness and direction (this is where we're all going, and this is how we're going to get there), people will assume that you don't know how to make it happen. You can only use *creative ambiguity* to entice a population out of its hole once, or maybe twice.
5 If you don't visualize failure and learn from it – then that's what you will deliver.

SECTION

4

Leaders need to be able to define and create a psychological contract that involves the nature of the goal, the level of risk and demonstrable commitment to survival of those who participate. I began to think that the collapse of Marks & Spencer may have been driven less by hubris, and more by the conscious or unconscious decision made by middle managers to satisfice, to go through the motions because corporate, courtier language – by the time it had cascaded down – no longer had any real meaning for employees.

The problem for leadership is that every day that it fails to identify, express in robust and everyday language, and solve the problems that are obvious to everyone, leadership stock devalues and decays, by the minute. And is very hard to recover. Another problem arises when leadership will not allow the development of a leadership franchise and get out of the way of the new, emergent leaders, instead of blocking them.

## Implications

1 KIR: Keep It Real. Don't use Potemkin language and concepts on real people, they will never take you seriously; use robust and real language to solve real problems.
2 KIS: Keep It Simple. Express where we are going, what we are going to do, how we are going to do it, and what different groups will need to contribute to make it happen.
3 Create and frame a context for engagement where you can invite volunteers to create new knowledge and capability.
4 Send your courtiers back to the front line. Frequently.

SECTION

4

# 5
# Creative Approaches
# and Tools

# 5.1

# Barefoot Knowledge

# Management

There is a consultants' story sometimes used to illustrate KM, involving two wilderness hikers resting in their tent, late at night in the Rocky Mountains. Individual A hears a bear growling in the vicinity, unzips their own sleeping-bag and pulls on a pair of training shoes. Individual B notices A's action and from within their own sleeping-bag asks why A has got up and is wearing training shoes. A answers to the effect that a grizzly bear is coming. B points out the futility of attempting to outrun a grizzly bear. A unzips the tent and, as he steps out, informs B that he doesn't have to outrun the grizzly, he only has to outrun B. At this point, the storyteller suggests that KM is about having a similar frame of mind. The problem is that many people are confusing KM with the acquisition and wearing of training shoes instead of being a means of delivering their business strategy! The term 'Barefoot KM' (without trainers) was designed to develop the kind of thinking necessary to emphasize that managing knowledge is a means to an end, and not a business strategy in its own right.

One of the key things to remember about KM is that it isn't about knowing everything, but about knowing where to look, and how to ask better questions. The key question that organizations need to ask themselves is not which software or training shoes to purchase, but what is KM actually supposed to do? One way of exploring this is to apply a Barefoot KM approach that enables an organization to develop an authentic approach to managing its knowledge within the context of its business strategy. So if KM is on the other side of the organization's coin to business strategy, then how do you go about applying a Barefoot KM approach to your organization?

1  *Preparation, context and technique.* It can be useful to be clear about the identity, membership and agreed business strategy (the full who, why, what, where, when and how) of the participants. The Creative Silence brainstorming technique using Post-its, needs to be introduced for creating and building ideas throughout the process. Finally, an overview map of the process needs to be explained.

2  *Visualize successful management of knowledge.* There are two similar entry approaches that can be taken here. One is to ask the group: 'How would we be able to tell if we were successfully managing our knowledge?' The other is to pose the scenario of the Prodigal's Return. The Prodigal's Return involves imagining returning to the organization having left and been headhunted back, and considering the question: 'On your return, what would tell you that we really had solved the issue of managing our knowledge?' In both cases teams are asked to visualize the symptoms of success: What would you notice? What would you see, feel, hear and taste in your environments? How would people behave and work together, differently?

3  *Create a successful knowledge strategy brochure.* By grouping the success symptoms into themes, these themes (aim for between three

and five only) are expressed in a series of statements. The idea is to visualize the kind of statements that you would love to be able to display in your reception foyer and reinforce in the way you work. Each statement begins with the keyword 'We' and expresses what could become the organization's knowledge principles and explains how we need to behave to make it happen.

4 *Develop and evaluate tactics to get to the vision.* This involves taking each success theme and brainstorming the obstacles and potential solutions that would overcome them, then positioning these within an Ease and Effect Matrix (EEM). At this point, the team can either just go for focusing on the top three solutions in terms of difficulty and impact and just do them; or sometimes teams like to take an intellectual step back, to review the solutions within the EEM to identify the top three themes across the EEM solutions and reconfigure these solutions as Banner Initiatives.

5 *Working with the Banner Initiatives.* Each Banner Initiative is laid out sequentially from start to finish in parallel, horizontal flows of Post-its, reviewed and resequenced to identify the following fundamental issues: Head, Heart and Graphical Working Model. Head items are those things that must be understood before we start, Heart items are those items that need to be in place so that people want to make it work, and Graphical Working Model items are about all those elements that can be represented in the form of a physical board game similar to Monopoly, so that everyone can check their understanding of how knowledge will be seamlessly integrated into work. The final part of playing with the Graphical Working Model is to identify the point at which we will be able to select an appropriate technology to facilitate our emerging approach to knowledge.

SECTION

5

## Implications

1 Your knowledge strategy and your business strategy are two sides of the same coin, moving in the same direction to deliver the same goal.

2 Barefoot KM is about involving the right people to develop an authentic approach to knowledge work that delivers your strategy without confusing KM with the acquisition of specific technologies.

3 If you cannot visualize success, you probably won't have any.

SECTION

5

## 5.2

# Predator's Mask

In 1998, Andy Grove of Intel published a book entitled *Only the Paranoid Survive*.[1] To reduce the text to its most simple and direct message, it said that you have two alternatives: be aware that a predator may appear and destroy your business; or be your own predator and be in charge of the type and timing of the attack. Grove's book and his concept are a useful start for organizations wrestling with the problem of knowledge management because, by implication, it forces individuals to wrestle with the problem of knowledge by thinking about the location and measure of value within the organization. Essentially, wherever the value is, that's also the location of the knowledge that's worth knowing.

One of the recent urban consulting myths about e-business implementation is that it is easier to sell an e-business strategy to an entrepreneur than to an MD of a £100 million turnover business. Everyone asks why that might be. The answer is that the entrepreneur started the business and has survived by understanding and extending the nature of the value (and hence the differentiating knowledge), its lifecycle and its key timings. The MD of the £100 million turnover business needs two days of facilitation with their top team to understand the value of the business, its location and potential timing. The problem is that the MD can't see the value of the facilitation, and doesn't want to pay for it when all they wanted was an e-business strategy. The problem is that if you don't understand the value within the business, and the location and lifecycle of the knowledge, the e-business strategy itself will fail.

So what can be done to understand the value of knowledge within the organization? There are two immediate 'P' approaches: Pyromaniac and Predator. Pyromaniac involves setting fire to the building or the organization and noting who runs into the flames to rescue which items. This could be expensive and involve Health and Safety issues. The second approach is Predator.

Predator is a five-stage scenario development exercise for: rediscovering your business, visualizing the organization's hidden value to identify the location of its competitive knowledge, anticipating market shifts in your competitive environment, and learning to do it to yourself, before they do.

SECTION

5

## So how does Predator work? What happens?

1 *Visualize the Predator.* The Predator exercise asks you to tap into the dark side of your innate paranoia to visualize an attacker who is not like you, who does not share any of your legacy emotions, technologies, customers, suppliers or associations about your business.

2 *Put on the Predator's mask to visualize the types of attacks/shifts in market.* Having developed the identity and motivations of your Predator, we then assume the Predator role to visualize the type

of attacks that could make your products or processes obsolete, severely reduce their market value, or chop up your value chain to make it unworkable.

3 *Do the Predator dance: structure the attack/market-shift strategy.* The emergent tactics of the Predator are then individually visualized and re-ordered as a complete, explicit strategy flow, in a sequence of set-piece attacks with specific objectives that neutralize and remove the sources of competitive knowledge.

4 *Anticipate the Predator's moves and timing: develop pre-emptive retaliation.* Participants review the Predator attack sequence and develop antidote tactics that pre-empt the Predator's attack strategy. These can be modelled within an EEM (Ease and Effect Matrix) to facilitate prioritization.

5 *Take off the Predator mask: review learning from Predator exercise.* This involves documenting participants' individual and group learning: what has surprised them, what have they learnt, and what new thing are they going to do as a result? The most consistent outcomes have been the realization that living within the 'box' of the organization has blinded everyone to the real 'potential' value that has become lost, and that the Predator strategy that they developed for themselves has identified the real knowledge assets and the need to exploit these consistently.

## Process and options

P1 At each stage, participants use Creative Silence Brainstorming to develop ideas, and present back to the facilitator or to parallel teams.

P2 It is advisable not to have more than three teams working concurrently, and no more than eight individuals in each team.

P3 The Predator Exercise can be cut down to three stages or the full process can be run. There are variants at each level.

SECTION

5

P4   A useful minimum-time exercise lasts two fairly rushed hours, a more useful session takes up to four hours. The shortest useful game has been 45 minutes, and the longest 72 hours.

P5   Useful prework can involve reading Sun Tsu's *Art of War*. Alternatively, a warm-up session introducing Sun Tsu's work and inviting participants to develop applications of his fundamental principles can be run without any preparation as a warm-up to the main event, lasting 90 minutes.

## Implications

1   Only the paranoid know where the real knowledge is, how much it's worth and how to hide it.

2   Thinking outside the box is rare. Thinking about destroying the box you inhabit in order to understand its limitations is even rarer.

3   Don't wait, become your own Predator. Put on the mask today, because tomorrow will not take care of itself.

## Note

1   Andy Grove, *Only the Paranoid Survive*, HarperCollins Business, 1998.

SECTION

5

## 5.3

# The Eternal

# Innovating Triangle

I suspect that as a child I was the one who shouted out the probable source of the conjurer's coins before they appeared out of my friends' ears. I must have ruined a few children's parties before I learnt to shut up and pretend not to notice what was really going on. It's this spirit of party-pooping that led to my capping a series of colleagues' workshop introductions all dutifully announcing their shared love of change, to find myself saying something quite to the contrary. I heard myself announce that I disliked change because it usually meant that the thing you least wanted to happen had come to pass. I hated change, but I loved transformation. Change is a relative term. Transformation however, requires radically rethinking the organization to deliver innovations and it involves understanding how to work with at least three different types of individual behaviour in order to create new forms of competitive knowledge and successfully take them to market.

I've always been fascinated by innovation, by the stories of innovators starving and fighting to promote their ideas, by the serendipitous nature of innovating and the romantic stories of success. But after a number of years of dabbling in the psychology of managing change to deliver innovation, I began to connect my experiences in a way that suggested that we needed a new model to explain the social dynamics of organizations.

These included:

1 *The reappearing 70% failure rate of systemic change initiative.* I tracked this statistic back to a 1972 TQM magazine, and have noticed its reappearance in different contexts by various authors. It is usually interpreted to suggest that change management is risky and requires effective planning and top management commitment.

2 *The largely identical content of serious books on change management.* Having implemented and participated in implementation initiatives that redesigned processes, integrated acquisitions and new technologies and refocused organizations, I began to notice that the content of these packaged approaches to change was largely identical. In other words, there was a central core of content that was about problem identification and solution in teams, and this tended to be managed in a standard way that might be called programme project management.

3 *Business process redesign tends to avoid redesigning the process of innovating within an organization.* Going back to the heydays of Business Process Reengineering (1995), I noticed that when consultant friends told the inside story behind publicized case studies featured within management literature, the actual benefits gained turned out to be marginal compared to those advertised in the literature. Similarly, when I reviewed the content of presentations made at BPR conferences, they tended (with very few exceptions) to be about transforming largely low-value, high-volume administrative

SECTION

5

processes and very, very rarely about transforming a process for innovating.

4 *Why do internal change agents have to leave the business?* My work and interest in the psychology of implementing change and leadership meant that I met many courageous individuals who decided to grasp the nettle, and led their charge in transforming their part of the business. But I also noticed that many of them left the organization once they felt that their work was done or mostly done.

So putting all this stuff together and reflecting, what seems to be going on? When I interviewed departing internal change agents, I discovered that their departure was due to several issues. First, that they had themselves changed by daring to break ranks to lead whilst others hung back to see whether it was going to be worth taking the risk of participation. This experience had changed their self-perception of who they themselves could choose to be, as opposed to the person whom the organization would license them to be. The second issue was that there was often a core management population within the organization that would never forgive them for daring to lead in their place. This core had long memories and tended to eat their dish of revenge when it was cold and our change agents didn't plan to stick around for the payback. If the literature of serious change management has a repetitive core content that is largely about programme project management and if change still tends to fail, then this is a piece of knowledge that is being unlearnt as quickly as it is being learnt, or perhaps it just cannot be learnt by some people. Maybe the literature itself is fine, but knowledge underlying the ability to manage change is not being integrated into the organizations' culture or way of working. If supposedly innovative business process redesign programmes are merely improving administrative activities, then there must therefore be something about organizations that is inimical to real change and innovation, that restricts process redesign to things that don't really matter. This connects with what we already know about organizations

SECTION

5

and individuals, that they both tend to change only when there is no alternative – not when an idea is intellectually interesting in itself.

Putting (1) to (4) together, Kazem Chaharbaghi of East London University Business School and I developed a model of Innovating Stereotypes that helped us to understand how different types of behaviour interact within organizations to support innovating. Later on I developed an Innovating Stereotypes Profile that would help individuals understand what was missing in their roles and their work, and help them to define what they needed to be more successful.

Essentially, we came to the conclusion that for innovating to occur within an organization you need three generic types of individual behaviour.

- *Creators.* Creators develop the ideas with the potential to create instability within organizations. They are the source of obsolescence. The moment an idea or prototype has worked, they tend to lose interest in it and want to move onto the next thing.
- *Stabilizors.* Stabilizors love managing the business as a system. They focus on controlling processes to reduce variation and improve on it. They always run a tight ship.
- *Implementors.* These are the entrepreneurs, the hungry, two-faced individuals who can speak both the language of the Creator and of the Stabilizor. They are the intermediaries who carry the Creator's prototype over to the Stabilizor. They keep a constant eye on the market, they recognize the emergent opportunity for ideas and work with the Creators to stabilize the prototype, and then sell it to the Stabilizors, working with them to develop workable versions and delivery systems.

If we look at the interactions between the Innovating Stereotypes, the Stabilizor is the ultimate brake on the Innovating process within an organization. They tend to inherit and reinforce the existing business formula, and they depend on apprenticeship development of their subordinates within existing functional knowledge structures to keep knowledge fractured and separate to the innovation process. They tend to focus on the familiar, ignoring those things that are outside their experience. They avoid ambiguity and uncertainty. Their biggest weakness is that they restrict creativity to the improvement of existing processes and products. Stabilizors must destroy all sources of variation and change within the organization. If given control of the business, they will always drive out the source of innovation and expel the Creators, who are the source of real innovation. The absence of Creators, the source of instability and crises, accordingly removes the need for Implementors, who have no role to fulfil, and ultimately produces stagnation. The Creators and Stabilizors despise each other: the Stabilizors despise the Creators because of the messes that they have to clear up after them; and the Creators despise the Stabilizors for optimizing and stabilizing technologies and processes which the Creators have already lost interest in. The Creators and Stabilizors need their translator and intermediary: the Implementor (whom neither really trust).

A key lesson is that we need to balance all three types of behaviour.

I have found this to be a useful model. The Innovating Stereotypes are extremes. Experience shows that everyone has components and relative proportions of all three Innovating Stereotypes in their behavioural portfolio, depending upon the limitations of their work environment and their natural work preferences. The idea of the Innovating Stereotypes has been turned into a practical diagnostic profile that compares the differences between the preferences and reality for each Innovating Stereotype in terms of type of work and work environment, identifying quantifiable shifts in how the individual would like their portfolio of relative Creator/Implementor/Stabilizor behaviours to be proportioned and the relative shifts required to move from actual to the preferred.

SECTION

5

| Innovating stereotype | Actual (within the limitations of the given environment and type of work) | Preferred (environment and type of work) | Stereotype shifts (Innovating tension) |
|---|---|---|---|
| Creator | 20% | 70% | +50% |
| Implementor | 15% | 25% | +10% |
| Stabilizor | 65% | 5% | −60% |

It has been interesting applying these as part of appraisals to help individuals understand how they feel about the work they do and the type of work they would prefer to be doing, and focusing on resolving the tension between the two. A classic and repetitive pattern in applying the Innovating Stereotypes Profile diagnostic to innovative teams has been the wish to be more creative (even though they were recruited to be innovative) but to significantly reduce the Stabilizor component of their Innovating Stereotypes Portfolio as in the example above, where the reduction of Stabilizor behaviour is by 60%, with a preferred portfolio increase of 50%, and 10% in Creator and Implementor behaviour. This has usually been due to the need to redesign their administrative support to allow them to get on with doing what they love, which is acting as Creator/Implementors.

You will find the Innovating Styles Profile in section 5.4.

SECTION

5

## Implications

1 If you have to build new processes, make sure that they are about innovating. If you don't have an explicit innovating process in your organization, then you are probably living off an old knowledge formula whose sell-by date is getting closer than you realize.

2 Build requisite variety into your organization; make sure that you have enough Creators, Implementors and Stabilizors in the right places.

3 Don't let your organization become swamped by one of the Innovating Stereotypes at the expense of the other two; you need them all to keep innovating.

## 5.4

# Innovating Styles Profile

**Workview profile**

Complete *this* profile first!

This part of the profile is designed to understand what you think about the work you currently do within your organization, and also how you would like to work.

Complete this profile in two phases: first, consider [a] work reality and then [b] personal preference.

In both phases you are asked to *select no more than 10 out of the 30 comments* that most closely complement the statements for work reality [a] 'In reality, work is about…', and personal work preferences [b] 'My personal work preference is about…'

1   Begin by circling 10 of your most preferred [a] statements out of the 30 offered.

2   Next, circle 10 of your most preferred [b] statements out of the 30 offered.

3   Finally, transfer the circles around your 10 [a] and 10 [b] statements onto the Workview Innovating Evaluation page.

| | |
|---|---|
| 1a [work reality]<br>1b [personal preference] | Is about making things happen quickly. |
| 2a [work reality]<br>2b [personal preference] | Is about moving on to the next idea. |
| 3a [work reality]<br>3b [personal preference] | Is about having the autonomy and opportunity to change procedures and organizations. |
| 4a [work reality]<br>4b [personal preference] | Is about managing an incremental process of continuous improvement. |
| 5a [work reality]<br>5b [personal preference] | Is about managing meetings to inform people on progress and next steps. |
| 6a [work reality]<br>6b [personal preference] | Is about playing with ideas that break new ground. |
| 7a [work reality]<br>7b [personal preference] | Is about managing change efficiently. |
| 8a [work reality]<br>8b [personal preference] | Is about trial and error. |
| 9a [work reality]<br>9b [personal preference] | Is about being able to distance yourself from immediate events to see the bigger picture. |
| 10a [work reality]<br>10b [personal preference] | Is about monitoring the performance of the business process. |
| 11a [work reality]<br>11b [personal preference] | Is about focusing attention on ensuring the efficient utilization of all assets within the organization. |
| 12a [work reality]<br>12b [personal preference] | Is about connecting the people with the ideas to the people who will have to make it work. |
| 13a [work reality]<br>13b [personal preference] | Is about being able to take someone else's idea and turn it into a reality. |

SECTION

5

| | |
|---|---|
| 14a [work reality]<br>14b [personal preference] | Is about being first to enter the market. |
| 15a [work reality]<br>15b [personal preference] | Is about doing new and different things. |
| 16a [work reality]<br>16b [personal preference] | Is about being interested in crazy ideas and interesting people. |
| 17a [work reality]<br>17b [personal preference] | Is about seeing other people's points of view. |
| 18a [work reality]<br>18b [personal preference] | Is about being disciplined enough to see the opportunity that someone else has missed. |
| 19a [work reality]<br>19b [personal preference] | Is about believing that without clear focus and disciplines, nothing novel can be achieved. |
| 20a [work reality]<br>20b [personal preference] | Is about it being OK to swim against the tide, against received common wisdom. |
| 21a [work reality]<br>21b [personal preference] | Is about breaking an overall picture into detailed steps. |
| 22a [work reality]<br>22b [personal preference] | Is about setting performance measures and targets. |
| 23a [work reality]<br>23b [personal preference] | Is about looking for further opportunities to optimize our existing products. |
| 24a [work reality]<br>24b [personal preference] | Is about starting again from scratch. |
| 25a [work reality]<br>25b [personal preference] | Is about having the freedom to plan your diary. |
| 26a [work reality]<br>26b [personal preference] | Is about constantly reviewing the performance of the competition. |
| 27a [work reality]<br>27b [personal preference] | Is about identifying and attacking fundamental, structural problems. |
| 28a [work reality]<br>28b [personal preference] | Is about making sure that the right people are doing the right work. |
| 29a [work reality]<br>29b [personal preference] | Is about making choices that appear to be complex to other people turn out to be very simple. |
| 30a [work reality]<br>30b [personal preference] | Is about ensuring that people stick to the documented procedures. |

SECTION

5

## Working environment profile

This is your *second* profile!

This part of the profile is designed to understand what you think about the environment you currently work within, and also the kind of environment in which you would like to work.

Complete this profile in two phases: first, consider [a] actual work environment and then [b] preferred work environment.

In both phases you are asked to *select no more than 10 out of 30 comments* that most closely complement the statements for work environments [a] In reality my work environment is one where...', and personal work environment preferences [b] 'My preferred work environment is one where...'

1 Begin by circling 10 of your most preferred [a] statements out of the 30 offered.
2 Next, circle 10 of your most preferred [b] statements out of the 30 offered.
3 Finally, transfer the circles around your 10 [a] and 10 [b] statements onto the Working Environment Innovating Evaluation page.

| | |
|---|---|
| 1a [actual work environment]<br>1b [personal preference] | Our processes for getting things done are accessible and can be modified to include what we've learnt. |
| 2a [actual work environment]<br>2b [personal preference] | It's OK to look beyond the immediate environment to look for signals of new emerging patterns. |
| 3a [actual work environment]<br>3b [personal preference] | Your contribution can be unique. |
| 4a [actual work environment]<br>4b [personal preference] | The customer's requirements determine what we deliver. |
| 5a [actual work environment]<br>5b [personal preference] | The public reception area provides an accurate impression of the way we work and who we really are. |

| | |
|---|---|
| 6a [actual work environment]<br>6b [personal preference] | There are no architectural barriers to movement and meetings, no large desks or formal office layout; there's room to play, build models, interact and capture ideas. |
| 7a [actual work environment]<br>7b [personal preference] | Decisions are taken at the correct management level. |
| 8a [actual work environment]<br>8b [personal preference] | You can determine what's important. |
| 9a [actual work environment]<br>9b [personal preference] | We take personal responsibility for delivering the agreed outcome. We are not here to watch the clock. |
| 10a [actual work environment]<br>10b [personal preference] | There is a clear chain of command and communication. |
| 11a [actual work environment]<br>11b [personal preference] | The way things look says the way we really are; what you see is what you get. |
| 12a [actual work environment]<br>12b [personal preference] | Serious thought has gone into making it possible to work intensively outside normal office routines and without interruptions, until the job is done. |
| 13a [actual work environment]<br>13b [personal preference] | The people you work with are diverse and interesting. It's OK to involve strangers. |
| 14a [actual work environment]<br>14b [personal preference] | It's OK to think deeply and realistically to anticipate all the obstacles to getting things done. |
| 15a [actual work environment]<br>15b [personal preference] | There are no organizational boundaries, you can network widely outside conventional disciplines and functions. |
| 16a [actual work environment]<br>16b [personal preference] | We can communicate accurately with each other on what we believe is missing, the level of risk and what needs to be done to remove or manage it. |
| 17a [actual work environment]<br>17b [personal preference] | IT is a complementary tool that can facilitate creativity, and is not seen as an end in itself. |
| 18a [actual work environment]<br>18b [personal preference] | There is a fundamental bedrock of strong, shared disciplines for communicating and getting things done. |

SECTION

5

| | |
|---|---|
| 19a [actual work environment]<br>19b [personal preference] | It's scary but fun to work on something that hasn't been done before. |
| 20a [actual work environment]<br>20b [personal preference] | It's OK to break out of routines. |
| 22a [actual work environment]<br>22b [personal preference | Managers and team leaders keep everyone focused on their tasks. |
| 23a [actual work environment]<br>23b [personal preference] | Limited time is prioritized and allocated for you. |
| 24a [actual work environment]<br>24b [personal preference] | You only get asked to work on critical issues that really matter. |
| 25a [actual work environment]<br>25b [personal preference] | Individuals are encouraged to develop personal mastery, to become the best in their field. |
| 26a [actual work environment]<br>26b [personal preference] | There are documented routines for every activity. |
| 27a [actual work environment]<br>27b [personal preference] | It's OK to take time to think outside the box. |
| 28a [actual work environment]<br>28b [personal preference] | The standards of individual performance are clearly defined to support the business processes. |
| 29a [actual work environment]<br>29b [personal preference] | It's OK to invent a crisis that hasn't yet appeared. |
| 30a [actual work environment]<br>30b [personal preference] | Although work may be routine, there is a strong sense of community. |

SECTION

5

## Workview innovating evaluation

| Name: | |
|---|---|

Transfer the 10 numbered statements in both [a] and [b] categories, by circling the [a] and [b] items and the C, I or S codes in the columns to the right.

Then add up the C, I or S codes and put the values in the boxes at the bottom of this matrix.

| WORKVIEW REALITY | | | | WORKVIEW PREFERENCE | | | |
|---|---|---|---|---|---|---|---|
| 1a | | I | | 1b | | I | |
| 2a | C | | | 2b | C | | |
| 3a | C | | | 3b | C | | |
| 4a | | | S | 4b | | | S |
| 5a | | | S | 5b | | | S |
| 6a | C | | | 6b | C | | |
| 7a | | | S | 7b | | | S |
| 8a | C | | | 8b | C | | |
| 9a | | I | | 9b | | I | |
| 10a | | | S | 10b | | | S |
| 11a | | | S | 11b | | | S |
| 12a | | I | | 12b | | I | |
| 13a | | I | | 13b | | I | |
| 14a | | I | | 14b | | I | |
| 15a | C | | | 15b | C | | |
| 16a | | I | | 16b | | I | |
| 17a | | I | | 17b | | I | |
| 18a | | I | | 18b | | I | |
| 19a | | I | | 19b | | I | |
| 20a | C | | | 20b | C | | |
| 21a | | I | | 21b | | I | |
| 22a | | | S | 22b | | | S |
| 23a | | | S | 23b | | | S |
| 24a | C | | | 24b | C | | |
| 25a | C | | | 25b | C | | |
| 26a | | | S | 26b | | | S |
| 27a | C | | | 27b | C | | |
| 28a | | | S | 28b | | | S |
| 29a | C | | | 29b | C | | |
| 30a | | | S | 30b | | | S |
| | | | | | | | |
| | C | I | S | | C | I | S |
| | (A) | (B) | (C) | | (D) | (E) | (F) |

SECTION

5

## Working environment innovating evaluation

Transfer the 10 numbered statements in both [a] and [b] categories, by circling the [a] and [b] items and the C, I or S codes in the columns to the right.

Then add up the C, I or S codes and put the values in the boxes at the bottom of this matrix.

| ACTUAL WORK ENVIRONMENT | | | | PREFERRED WORK ENVIRONMENT | | | |
|---|---|---|---|---|---|---|---|
| 1a | | I | | 1b | | I | |
| 2a | C | | | 2b | C | | |
| 3a | C | | | 3b | C | | |
| 4a | | | S | 4b | | | S |
| 5a | | | S | 5b | | | S |
| 6a | C | | | 6b | C | | |
| 7a | | | S | 7b | | | S |
| 8a | C | | | 8b | C | | |
| 9a | | I | | 9b | | I | |
| 10a | | | S | 10b | | | S |
| 11a | | | S | 11b | | | S |
| 12a | | I | | 12b | | I | |
| 13a | | I | | 13b | | I | |
| 14a | | I | | 14b | | I | |
| 15a | C | | | 15b | C | | |
| 16a | | I | | 16b | | I | |
| 17a | | I | | 17b | | I | |
| 18a | | I | | 18b | | I | |
| 19a | | I | | 19b | | I | |
| 20a | C | | | 20b | C | | |
| 21a | | I | | 21b | | I | |
| 22a | | | S | 22b | | | S |
| 23a | | | S | 23b | | | S |
| 24a | C | | | 24b | C | | |
| 25a | C | | | 25b | C | | |
| 26a | | | S | 26b | | | S |

| 27a | C | | | | 27b | C | | | |
|-----|---|---|---|---|-----|---|---|---|---|
| 28a | | | | S | 28b | | | | S |
| 29a | C | | | | 29b | C | | | |
| 30a | | | | S | 30b | | | | S |
| | | | | | | | | | |
| | C | I | | S | | C | I | | S |
| | (G) | (H) | | (I) | | (J) | (K) | | (L) |

## Innovating evaluation

Transfer the C, I and S values from boxes A to L on the previous two pages onto this page, then add up the columns, creating fractions of 20.

Transform these fractions into percentages (multiplying by 5) and put these into the highlighted boxes.

Finally, compare the Actual and Preferred values in the 'CIS' boxes.

Ask yourself the meaning of any shifts in values for either 'C, I or S' from one side, to the other.

| WORKVIEW REALITY | | | WORKVIEW PREFERENCE | | |
|---|---|---|---|---|---|
| Creator (A) | Implementor (B) | Stabilizor (C) | Creator (D) | Implementor (E) | Stabilizor (F) |
| Creator (G) | Implementor (H) | Stabilizor (I) | Creator (J) | Implementor (K) | Stabilizor (L) |
| Actual work environment | | | Preferred work environment | | |
| A + G =/20 | B + H =/20 | C + I =/20 | D + J =/20 | E + K =/20 | F + L =/20 |
| % | % | % | % | % | % |
| | | | +/- Creator | +/- Implementor | +/- Stabilizor |

Compare actual vs. preference:  A+G:D+J  B+H:E+K  C+I:F+L

---

## 5.5

# Dream/Unpack/Engage

---

You'll probably never know what you know until someone asks you a good question. The role of leadership in driving innovating behaviour is largely about building a framework out of good questions which together create the opportunity to build and integrate new knowledge with the potential to deliver new market value.

To paraphrase once again an old change management joke: how many consultants does it take to change a light-bulb? The answer is that the number of consultants is immaterial, the light-bulb itself has got to want to change. Focused innovation is about wanting to do something different and knowing how to engage the right people in the right way.

Three stories. First, the science fiction story which I can't, unfortunately, source, set in the early period of the Cold War. A team of scientists is taken to a top secret, secure location and shown a clandestine film of a secret device which the enemy is developing. The inventor is shown controlling what appears to be a form of anti-gravity device. The team is given unlimited resources. Within six months, they surpass the reported performance of the original device. They return to the secure location to celebrate, and are introduced to the 'inventor' featured in the original, clandestine film. They have obviously been hoaxed and initially feel very angry. They calm down when the director of the project points out their achievement: they have done something that was originally believed to be impossible. Visualization is part of the psychology of the possible. If we believe something is possible, we can anticipate the obstacles and work to make it happen.

Second, in my first lean production implementation within an automotive assembly plant, I was asked to set up a suggestions scheme. I thought I'd be clever. One of the major criticisms that contributors of ideas make about in-house suggestion schemes is the time-lag between submitting an idea and getting a response as to its potential utility. I thought I'd be smart and apply some Shingo-like logic to the one I was going to set up, by building the success criteria into the paperwork itself so that contributors would be able to apply a weighted scoring approach to their own idea, and only submit it if it reached a certain threshold. I assumed that this would ensure that we only got to work on ideas that had real impact. I promised a turnaround on reception and escalation to the production manage-ment team of five working days. What eventually happened amazed even me. It seemed at first that I hadn't pitched the weighted-scoring threshold high enough. I had over 200 ideas on my desk by the third day of the launch. To control my mounting panic, I began to code and position the ideas onto a brown-paper, crudely-drawn map of the assembly process that I had drawn earlier. I began to notice that there were some interesting clusters emerging around certain locations, like bottlenecks within the process. This either meant that employees at those locations were unhappy or we had some obvious problems. As I stepped back further from the model, a revolutionary thought

SECTION

5

struck me: there was no point in making this process better, it was full of weaknesses, and improvements at one point would always be diminished by weaknesses somewhere else. It was time to do something drastic, and to do it now.

The third story involved coming into contact with an overarching technique for all lean production techniques, the big daddy of them all: *hoshin kanri*, or policy deployment. This involved the considered application or deployment of a host of minor techniques within an overall matrix across the whole business process. It was at this point that I began to realize that *kaizen* (usually translated as 'ongoing improvement involving everyone') was not what I was seeing at world-class manufacturing plants in Japan. UK adapters usually tried to involve everyone in innovating and made a mess of it. What policy deployment seemed to do was to identify where the weaknesses were in the overall business process, and selectively apply techniques to improve them significantly in a prioritized sequence.

The complementary lessons from these three stories:

1   Make it clear where you are going. Dream a dream that's different. It probably doesn't matter if it's crazy, as long as it's different. If you cannot visualize a different future, then all you can get is more of the same.

2   Work out where you need the innovation. This will involve constructing a model of your key business process, and identifying significant weaknesses. Alternatively, you can visualize a dramatically different set of outcomes for your business, and then review that model to see where change needs to be. Another approach is to take the aspirational goal (whatever it is) and turn it into a problem statement along the lines of 'we don't believe we can deliver the aspirational goal X, by Y' and to unpack it by repeatedly asking the question 'Why?', capturing answers on Post-its to build a Why/Why diagram that gives you a rough cut of the dependencies involved and, ultimately, the potential root causes that need to be attacked. Without some map or model of where you need the innovation, you have no context for engaging crea-

tivity amongst individuals and teams, and will be unable to answer the question, 'What kind of innovations do you want?' And the innovators will just stay in the background, keeping their powder dry because they know you're not serious.

3 Have a clear plan of engagement, an innovation plan for individuals and existing functional groups. Be clear about which types of innovation are best driven by existing structures and teams, and where you are going to invite individuals to participate and contribute their own ideas. Remember, individuals tend to be more creative than teams; teams are great at making things happen and spotting the gaps.

4 Model what's going on outside the box. Maintain an external view of the potential, serendipitous impact of innovations from outside the organization, on the way things are done. We tend to look inside the business and ignore those vectors, or emerging items of new knowledge, which have the potential, once connected, to transform the way we do our business. We may choose to reduce risk by not being first adapters, but our timing in following the first adapter wave could be critical, and we could also connect technologies and ideas in novel ways.

5 Continuously educate everyone about the dreams, the model and its opportunities for innovation within it, the plan for engaging individuals, functions and teams, and the potential nature of alternative scenarios that could replace the way we choose to do business.

SECTION

5

## Implications

1 Cheat. (Pretend the impossible is possible, then build a bridge to get there.)
2 Model and Move. (Find a way to represent the nature of the problems within the situation and the way you'd like it to be, and don't be afraid to look at the model in a new way by adopting a different perspective.)
3 Connect and Steal. (What does the problem remind you of? Who's already solved this problem within a different context?)
4 Play and Reverse. (Take the model apart; break it, reassemble it; run the assembly process backwards – what do you notice about redundancy?)

SECTION

5

# 6
# Startgame/Endgame

It's probably appropriate to attempt some kind of conclusion to this book. At the point of writing, it feels as though this is an endgame in chess, the final moves that finish the game. And yet I'd like to think this could just the beginning, and if it is a game, that we've both enjoyed not only playing it but also disagreeing with the implications at the end of each chapter.

Before I get to the finish, it's probably appropriate to say something that fits the title of this book: *The Knowledge Activist's Handbook*. The associations begin with the familiar stereotype of the single-issue political activist whose lone voice tells unsavoury truths or offers startling, alternative perspectives and narratives about topics that we'd much prefer to think could only be seen only one way or not at all.

Although I have always had minor doubts about the experiential learning model (like, why only four types of learning? And why four discrete stages and not, say, six?), it is the other partial source of my use of the word 'activist' in the title and this deserves some consideration.

In retrospect, I began to realize that although all four learning styles appear in the way the chapters were written, with the Reflector reviewing and observing, the Theorist drawing conclusions, and the Pragmatist experimenting: there was also a significant chunk of the Activist stereotype in my approach to this book that underlines the choice of title. To quote:

> *Activists involve themselves fully and without bias in new experiences. They enjoy the here and now and are happy to be dominated by immediate experiences. They are open-minded, not sceptical, and this tends to make them enthusiastic about anything new.*[1]

SECTION

6

Knowledge management has been a boon to natural enthusiasts, and it is this natural enthusiasm and joy in diving deep into the refreshing unknown that keeps us all interested in the topic, that makes it possible to participate in engrossing conversations with complete strangers that we don't want to end. Whilst all four stereotypes need each other, it is this enthusiasm that makes it all worthwhile.

Ultimately, I realize that my overall message is that the management of knowledge is personal, it has to do with living and learning, developing a personal view and building tools from experience that make a difference. Whilst I might have to admit that knowledge management is the deliberate management of knowledge to deliver specific outcomes, I confess I have a sneaking regard for what I might call the activist, or the Wackford Squeers school of knowledge management. This approach deliberately emphasizes experience and practise after some preliminary, minor interest in abstract theory, as headteacher Squeers explained to Nicholas Nickleby:

> 'When he has learned that bottiney means a knowledge of plants, he goes and knows 'em. That's our system, Nickleby: what do you think of it?'
>
> 'It's a very useful one at any rate,' answered Nicholas significantly.[2]

And so, if I attempt to synthesize the synthesis, I find the following themes appearing and reappearing:

1. The time-based nature of competitive knowledge, and the increasing importance of managing the timing of knowledge around mobilization. Remember, boredom is your friend; if you find the knowledge you live by boring, move on.
2. The importance of alienation, of developing an alienated identity that promotes creativity and realism that is often taken for cynicism. We all need the ability to be refugees from a lost society, and readers of their texts to understand what's at risk and what is missing in our present.
3. The importance of leaders understanding their role as creators of the framework for engagement that makes it possible for individuals and teams to participate in innovating behaviour that creates and mobilizes new behaviours and makes work meaningful.

SECTION

6

4 The need to continually search for 'lost' and broken cause-and-effect models. Especially when they only exist tacitly in the heads of our chief executives.

I am also struck by my title to this concluding chapter. I came up with endgame spontaneously (the concluding stage in a chess game) and found it depressing as a title (though accurate in this case), and I had to change it to suggest that maybe, for reader and author, this could be just another beginning.

## Notes

1 Peter Honey and Alan Mumford, *The Manual of Learning Styles*, Peter Honey, 1992.
2 Charles Dickens, *Nicholas Nickleby*, Penguin, 1978.

SECTION

6

# Index